THE AUTHOR

Brian O'Kane is the managing director of Tree Press, an international developer and publisher of enterprise training and support materials.

A chartered accountant by training, Brian has edited the professional member magazines of the Institute of Chartered Accountants in England & Wales and the Association of Chartered Certified Accountants.

With co-director Ron Immink, he has written **Starting Your Own Business: A Workbook, TENBizPlan: Dynamic Business Planning for Start-ups** and the **Steps to Entrepreneurship** series, as well as many magazine articles. He is also the webmaster for **www.startingabusinessinbritain.com**.

ABOUT THE AUTHOR

STARTING A BUSINESS IN BRITAIN

Brian O'Kane

Linked to
www.startingabusinessinbritain.com

First published in Great Britain in 2003 by
Virgin Books Ltd
Thames Wharf Studios, Rainville Road,
London W6 9HA.

A catalogue record of this book is
available from the British Library.

ISBN 0 7535 0820 6

Although the author and publisher have taken every care to
ensure that the information published in this book is correct at
the time of going to press, neither can take any responsibility
for any loss or damage caused to any person as a result of acting
on, or refraining from acting on, any information published
herein. Professional advice should be obtained before entering
into any legally binding commitments.

Printed by CPD, Wales.

CONTENTS

Preface   vii

Dedication   ix

1: Getting Started   1
   The Stages in a Start-up   2
   Are You Suited to Life as an Entrepreneur?   4
   Start Your Own Business Courses   8
   Incubators   9
   Start Early!   10
   Start-up Alternatives   10

2: Researching Your Idea   11
   Market Research   13
   Sources of Information   27
   Interpreting Research Results   31
   The Final Question   31

3: Writing a Business Plan   33
   The Purpose of a Business Plan   34
   Who Should Write Your Business Plan?   37
   How Long Should Your Business Plan Be?   38
   Figures   38
   A Standard Business Plan Format   41
   How a Financier Reads a Business Plan   49
   Writing a Business Plan   53

4: Financing Your Start-up   **55**

Equity   56
Debt   59
Dealing with Banks   63
Other Finance   66

5: Support for Start-ups in England   **67**

Accountants   69
Business Angels   70
Business Plans   71
Community & Rural Development   71
Competitions   72
Consultants   73
Co-operatives   74
Debt   74
E-Business   75
Enterprise Support   75
Equity   76
Franchises   77
Grants   77
Incubator   78
Information   79
Intellectual Property   81
Inwards Investment   81
Legal   82
Marketing   82
Mentoring   83
Minorities & Disabilities   83
Networking   84
Policy   85
Publications   85
R&D   86
Regulator & Standards   86
Social Economy   87
Start-Up Training   87
Training   88

Website   89
Women   90
Young Enterprise   90

6: Support for Start-ups in Scotland   93
Accountants   93
Business Angels   94
Business Plans   94
Community & Rural Development   94
Competitions   95
Consultants   95
Co-operatives   95
Debt   95
E-Business   96
Enterprise Support   96
Equity   96
Franchises   97
Grants   97
Incubator   97
Information   97
Intellectual Property   99
Inwards Investment   100
Legal   100
Marketing   100
Mentoring   100
Networking   100
Policy   101
Publications   101
R&D   101
Regulator & Standards   102
Social Economy   102
Start-Up Training   102
Training   103
Website   103
Women   105
Young Enterprise   105

7: Support for Start-ups in Wales   **107**

Accountants   107
Business Angels   108
Business Plans   108
Community & Rural Development   108
Competitions   108
Consultants   109
Co-operatives   109
Debt   109
E-Business   110
Enterprise Support   110
Equity   110
Franchises   110
Grants   111
Incubator   111
Information   111
Intellectual Property   113
Inwards Investment   113
Legal   113
Marketing   113
Mentoring   114
Minorities & Disabilities   114
Networking   114
Policy   114
Publications   115
R&D   115
Regulator & Standards   115
Social Economy   116
Start-Up Training   116
Training   116
Website   117
Women   118
Young Enterprise   118

8: Support for Start-ups in Northern Ireland   119

Accountants   119
Business Angels   120
Business Plans   120
Community & Rural Development   120
Competitions   120
Consultants   121
Debt   121
E-Business   122
Enterprise Support   122
Equity   122
Franchises   122
Grants   122
Incubator   123
Information   123
Intellectual Property   125
Inwards Investment   125
Legal   125
Marketing   125
Mentoring   126
Networking   126
Policy   126
Publications   127
R&D   127
Regulator & Standards   127
Social Economy   127
Start-Up Training   128
Training   128
Website   128
Women   130
Young Enterprise   130

9: EU Support for Start-ups in Britain   **131**
   Direct Assistance   131
   Indirect Assistance   132

10: Implementation   **133**
   Bank Accounts   133
   Legal Structure   135
   Taxation   137
   Advisers   145
   Accounting System   147
   Quality Certification   149

Directory of Sources of Support   **151**

PREFACE

Starting a Business in Britain is based on my best-selling book, **Starting a Business in Ireland**, which struck a chord with the Irish public right from its launch in 1993.

I met Robert Craven, series editor for business titles at Virgin Books, at an Institute of Business Advisers conference in Coventry in late 2001. It was he who spotted the opportunity to adapt a successful formula to UK needs. With Kirstie Addis, commissioning editor, he championed the project to fruition.

THE BOOK

Starting a business is frustrating, time-consuming and difficult – I know, because I have done it – but it can also be highly satisfying and enjoyable.

This book is designed to do two things:

- Take you step-by-step through the stages in going into business for yourself

- Help you to identify, from the many organisations that provide assistance to entrepreneurs, which are likely to be appropriate to your needs.

The chapters are arranged to take you through the various stages:

- Deciding whether you have what it takes (**Chapter 1**)

- Researching your idea (**Chapter 2**)

- Writing a business plan (**Chapter 3**)

- Raising money to set up your business (**Chapter 4**)

- Getting help from EU, Government and other agencies (**Chapters 5, 6, 7, 8 and 9**)

- Getting your business up and running (**Chapter 10**).

The **Directory of Sources of Support** provides information (including contact details) for the many organisations identified in the text that may be of use to you as you go through the stages of starting your own business.

THE WEBSITE

A companion website to this book is available at **www.startingabusinessinbritain.com**. There, you will find all the information from the **Directory of Sources of Support**, updated regularly, plus many other resources of benefit to entrepreneurs and small businesses. I hope that you will find it useful and I look forward to your feedback.

I have enjoyed writing this book. I hope it is of help to you, the reader, as you take your first steps on your journey. Good luck!

Brian O'Kane
April 2003

DEDICATION

Although the work of writing is essentially a solitary act, a book is never written alone. For their contribution to **Starting a Business in Britain**, I would like to thank:

- Robert Craven, series editor, and Kirstie Addis, commissioning editor, at Virgin Books for championing this project

- Ron Immink, my business partner and co-author on many other projects, for his unfailing cheerfulness and advice

- My wife, Rita, without whose constant support and encouragement little would be possible – or worthwhile.

1

GETTING STARTED

For some people, starting their own business is as obvious as the nose on their face. For others, it is a risk not to be contemplated.

For you, it is an idea in the back of your mind, one you cannot get rid of. You may already know what kind of business you want to be in. What you want from this book are a few short cuts to help you get there faster and with fewer problems.

On the other hand, you may simply be toying with the idea still, unsure of which direction to take. You are hoping that this book will present you with a ready-formed solution. In fact, you must provide your own solution but this book can help by showing you how to research an idea to make sure that it is viable.

The important thing is to take the time to plan your start-up carefully. Over half of all start-ups fail within the first three years – mainly due to lack of planning.

Starting a Business in Britain aims to give you a structure for your planning.

THE STAGES IN A START-UP

The stages involved in starting a business include:

- Deciding whether you have the right temperament to start (and persevere with) your own business

- Finding an idea

- Doing the market research – this involves finding out about your customers, your competition, how you will make your product or deliver your service, what price to charge, where your business will be located, how to market your product/service, what staff you require and with what skills and so on (**Chapter 2**)

- Writing a business plan – this draws together all the work you have done (**Chapter 3**)

- Finding the necessary money – since it's likely you won't have enough of your own capital to start, you'll have to raise money elsewhere (**Chapter 4**)

- Identifying and accessing sources of assistance – as **Chapters 5, 6, 7, 8** and **9** and the **Directory of Sources of Support** show, there are hundreds of organisations dedicated to helping small businesses get started

- Implementing your plan – this is where you put your plan into action (**Chapter 10**).

Sometimes, in practice, these stages will not follow in the order above; in other cases, you will have to double back, perhaps even several times, to adjust the results of a stage because of new information you find out later.

For instance, your idea might be to make a product and sell it in your own neighbourhood. After doing your market research, you write your business plan and look for money on this basis but, as you proceed, you find that there is a national demand for the product. To supply it, you need to plan on a larger scale and need more money – so you revise your plans and finances accordingly.

STAGES IN STARTING A BUSINESS

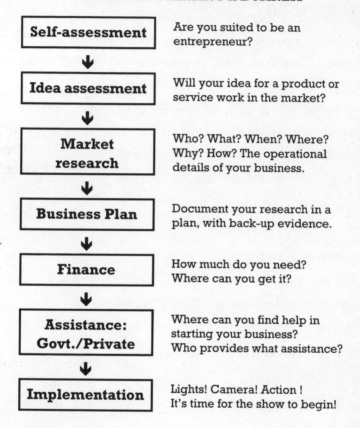

Self-assessment	Are you suited to be an entrepreneur?
Idea assessment	Will your idea for a product or service work in the market?
Market research	Who? What? When? Where? Why? How? The operational details of your business.
Business Plan	Document your research in a plan, with back-up evidence.
Finance	How much do you need? Where can you get it?
Assistance: Govt./Private	Where can you find help in starting your business? Who provides what assistance?
Implementation	Lights! Camera! Action! It's time for the show to begin!

But all the stages must be completed – skip even one and you risk failure!

ARE YOU SUITED TO LIFE AS AN ENTREPRENEUR?

Sadly, there is no fail-safe method of becoming a successful entrepreneur. International research shows that successful entrepreneurs have:

- Strong needs for control and independence
- Drive and energy
- Self-confidence
- A point of view of money as a measure of performance
- A tolerance of ambiguity and uncertainty
- A sense of social responsibility

and that they are good at:

- Problem-solving
- Setting (and achieving) goals and targets
- Calculated risk-taking
- Committing themselves for the long term
- Dealing with failure
- Using feedback
- Taking the initiative
- Seeking personal responsibility
- Tapping and using resources
- Competing against self-imposed standards.

How do *you* measure on these criteria? Be honest with yourself. Use the exercise on the next page to help you assess yourself.

YOUR SUITABILITY AS AN ENTREPRENEUR
Score yourself on these points – from 1 (weak) to 10 (strong)

	1	2	3	4	5	6	7	8	9	10
Need for control/independence										
Drive and energy										
Self-confidence										
Money to measure performance										
Tolerate ambiguity/uncertainty										
Sense of social responsibility										
Problem-solving										
Setting (and achieving) goals										
Calculated risk-taking										
Committing for the long term										
Dealing with failure										
Using feedback										
Taking the initiative										
Seeking personal responsibility										
Tapping and using resources										
Self-imposed standards										

Very few entrepreneurs can lay claim to all of these characteristics. Making the most of your best characteristics and using ingenuity (including the skills of others) to bridge the gaps is perhaps the most frequently encountered entrepreneurial characteristic of all!

However, despite the great variety of people who end up as business-owners, probably the most important personal characteristic for an entrepreneur is determination.

It's easy to start a business; it's more difficult to keep it going. When you are faced with long hours, with working through nights and weekends, with extended periods away from your family, and with financial worries, the thought of a secure, permanent, and pensionable job is tempting. Determination is what will see you through these lows, until you break through to success!

You should also consider your general state of health. Both the physical and mental stresses of running your own business can be very great. If you are driven to a state of collapse by the experience, you may leave your spouse/partner and family much more exposed financially than would be the case if you were in a secure job with benefits attached.

You should be aware of the part your spouse/partner and family will play in achieving your ambition of becoming an entrepreneur. Are they as committed as you are? Are they as willing to accept the lows as the highs? Without their support, you will find it difficult to start and develop your business. If they are actively pulling against you, quit now!

Part of the experience of running your own business is learning to apply the appropriate personal resource at the right time. For example, deciding to become an exporter at a time when your resources – foreign language skills, contacts, and finances – are not adequate is to misuse an opportunity that might lead to success in other circumstances. A touch of realism instead would have revealed the impracticality of your plan.

So the first thing you should do when thinking about starting a business is to conduct a rigorous self-assessment:

- What skills and experience do you have?

- What training do you need?

- What characteristics do you have that help (or hinder) you?

- Why do you want to start a business?

Write down the answers – it's not as easy to fudge uncomfortable answers in writing.

Then write your own application for the position of managing director and general *factotum* of your proposed business. Give your application to a friend not noted for their tact and wait for the laughs. You need to be able to see yourself as others see you.

Are your keyboard and literary skills really up to sending out customer letters and writing marketing blurbs? Perhaps you excel in production and technical innovation? Maybe you need to acquire other skills? If so, can you get by with a little training for yourself or should you buy in these skills on a freelance basis as and when required?

Will you need a management team, or are there family members who are sufficiently committed to help (and capable of doing so)? What will hiring all these people do to your costs?

Salaries usually represent a high percentage of costs in a small business. You need to be realistic about how many people you need, and how many you can afford – and what you do about the difference.

In terms of your business skills, you should consider, in addition to management experience, actual contacts and sales leads, as these are the concrete beginnings of your trading. If you plan to supply other retailers or manufacturers, you will be hoping to establish several guaranteed sales contracts before you finally start trading. If you are leaving employment to set up this kind of business, check that your employment contract allows you to canvass business on your own account (and time) while still an employee.

You should read this chapter again in a year's time. Why? Because you will only begin to discover the extent of your personal resources as you go along. Starting your own business will not only lead you to find hidden resources within yourself, but will build up existing strengths. It may also, of course, cause you to recognise unsuspected weaknesses, but recognising them is the first step towards correcting them.

START YOUR OWN BUSINESS COURSES

This book is designed to help you through the early stages of starting a business. For further guidance, or for the comfort of meeting like-minded people who are about to embark on the same adventure, consider a Start Your Own Business course.

These courses can be useful because they draw together all the aspects of running a business – it is often easy to ignore those tasks that bore you or for which you feel ill equipped. Another advantage of attending a course is that you get to know advisers who may be useful to contact later with queries.

Many adult education centres run Start Your Own Business courses during the winter evenings. Other courses are available commercially. See **Chapters 5** (England), **6** (Scotland), **7** (Wales), and **8** (Northern Ireland) for course providers in your region.

How Do You Choose the Right Course?

Before you book a place on a course, meet the organisers. Ask about the backgrounds of the presenters. Those who run their own business or who, like many accountants and other professionals, make their living from advising entrepreneurs are the best bet.

Ask about the success rate of the course in establishing new businesses. Ask about the success rate of those businesses after two or three years. Remember that the average failure rate of new businesses is very high. But, it need not apply to you, if you plan your start-up carefully.

Make an effort to find people who have completed any courses you are considering, and talk to them. They are in the best position to know whether what they learnt on the course actually was of use in practice. Their answers will tell you whether you should take a place on the course.

If You Can't Attend a Course

If you cannot participate in a Start Your Own Business course, try to attend some of the seminars on specific aspects of enterprise development and small business management presented from time to time by the banks and other organisations. These are aimed at reducing the fall-out rate of business start-ups and are usually open to the public (sometimes for a fee). Watch the newspapers for details.

Otherwise, read as widely as you can in the area of enterprise and business start-ups. There are plenty of good books, and newspapers and magazines regularly publish special features that give useful advice.

INCUBATORS

Perhaps, instead of merely a training programme, what you need is a push-start. Here an 'incubator' can help. An incubator is a programme/facility, usually focused on technology businesses, that encourages the faster development of a new business by providing a range of supports from workspace to finance to administrative assistance (and training, where necessary) in order to free up the entrepreneur to concentrate on the business alone.

Sometimes, the term 'incubator' is used loosely to cover mere provision of workspace – if you're offered incubation workspace, check what else is included. See **Chapters 5** (England), **6** (Scotland), **7** (Wales), and **8** (Northern Ireland) for incubators in your region.

START EARLY!

You're never too young to start thinking about enterprise and running your own business. Even if you're still in school or at college, there are programmes designed to attract you towards the notion of self-employment and to help you begin to gain the necessary skills. See **Chapters 5** (England), **6** (Scotland), **7** (Wales), and **8** (Northern Ireland) for programmes in your region.

START-UP ALTERNATIVES

Of course, it's not always necessary to start a business from scratch. Company brokers can help you to identify and buy a suitable business, whose owner lacks the capital or enthusiasm to develop it further.

Another alternative is to buy into a franchise – replicating an already-proven business model. McDonald's, Domino's Pizza, Budget Rent-a-Car and O'Brien's Irish Sandwich Bars are examples of well-known franchises, though there many more.

If you do go down the route of buying an existing business or a franchise, make sure that you take professional advice before making any financial or legal commitment. And continue to read the rest of this book, since you will still need to plan for the development of your business. See **Chapters 5** (England), **6** (Scotland), **7** (Wales), and **8** (Northern Ireland) for sources of information on franchising in your region.

2

RESEARCHING YOUR IDEA

After considering your own capacity to run a business (see **Chapter 1**), you next need to ask yourself whether a market exists for your product or service. The market may be incredibly tough to break into but, as long as it exists, you can fight for your share of it. If there is no market at all for your product or service, your business is clearly a non-starter.

You are not yet attempting to measure the size or location of the market, or to distinguish its characteristics. What you want are the answers to the following questions:

- Do others already offer the same product or service as I intend to offer?

- Is my product/service an improvement on what already exists?

- What evidence is there that customers want to buy my improved product/service?

If your product/service is new to the market, you need to ask:

- What evidence is there that the market wants to buy this product/service?
- What evidence is there that the market is aware of its need for my product/service?

You may be able to find answers to these questions quite easily. For example, the market for ready-mixed concrete is quite visible but it is dominated by a few big companies. So the question here quickly changes from whether a market exists to whether it is feasible to enter that market when there are already strong competitors in place.

On the other hand, the inventor of a solar-powered bicycle might have more difficulty assessing the existence of a market. All the cyclists he talks to may tell him that they only cycle for the exercise value, since they cannot depend on sufficient sun to make any difference to the energy they must expend in cycling. They might have no interest in any source of power beyond their own muscles. Yet, in environmentally conscious (and sunnier) countries that encourage the use of a bicycle and/or solar power, the product could be greeted with cries of delight and massive demand. However, if the inventor does not know where to look, he or she may never get their business off the ground.

This quick feasibility review will tell you whether it's worth progressing to more formal market research, or whether you should go back to the drawing board to think of a new product or service.

MARKET RESEARCH

Once you have provided yourself with proof – not just a gut feeling – of the existence of the market (see *Sources of Information* on page 27), you can move on to more detailed research. Analysing the nature of the market, competition and customer base will tell you whether your idea is feasible. The information you compile will allow you to develop your business plan in more detail.

Although a professional market research company will conduct research for you, at a price, you can often do your own research without too much difficulty, time or cost.

In collecting information during this research stage, remember that, as well as satisfying yourself, you may have to prove to outside investors that your figures and findings are valid. For this reason, independent proof is worth collecting wherever you can find it. Sources include:

- Talking to potential customers and even competitors

- Questionnaires and surveys

- Official government statistics or statistics compiled by trade associations and consumer bodies.

You need to sift carefully through the information you collect:

- To understand the business you are in

- To work out the size and location of the market for your product/service

- To build up a profile of your customers and their needs

- To understand how competition operates in your market

- To establish a reasonable price for your product/service – one at which your customers will buy

- To forecast sales – both volume and value

- To establish the cost of making your product or delivering your service – and how it will be done – as well as the profit margins you can expect

- To establish the investment needed to start your business

- To decide what form your business must take.

MARKET RESEARCH

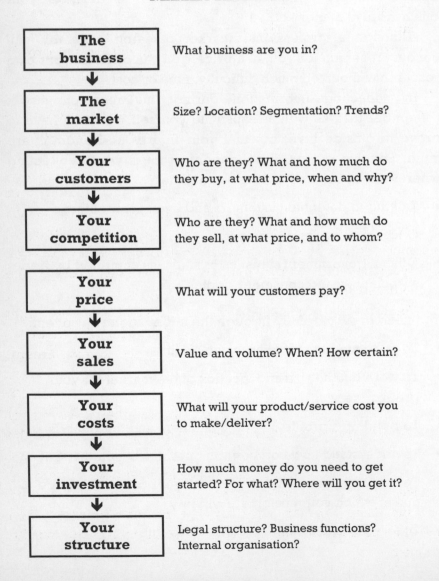

The business	What business are you in?
The market	Size? Location? Segmentation? Trends?
Your customers	Who are they? What and how much do they buy, at what price, when and why?
Your competition	Who are they? What and how much do they sell, at what price, and to whom?
Your price	What will your customers pay?
Your sales	Value and volume? When? How certain?
Your costs	What will your product/service cost you to make/deliver?
Your investment	How much money do you need to get started? For what? Where will you get it?
Your structure	Legal structure? Business functions? Internal organisation?

What Is Your Business?

This may seem an obvious question, one not worth asking, but setting it down in writing may provide a useful reference exercise.

For example, Wedgwood is not in the business of providing everyday chinaware. Despite the fact that it produces plates, bowls and vases, it does not compete with the producer of the everyday cup and saucer that you find in the supermarket or department store. Rather, it is in the international market for luxury goods and special occasion gifts. It will look to growth trends in these luxury markets, mainly overseas, rather than to growth in chinaware sales generally.

In contrast, a contract carpet-cleaning business in Birmingham provides a very specific service in the city, or possibly even only in one area of the city.

Be aware that if you are a manufacturer, you are a manufacturer, not a retailer. You may sell your product to or through a dealer, but you are not a dealer, nor are you selling direct to the public. To try to be more than you are can spell doom for a small business, because your business may not have the resources and you may not have the necessary skills to take on your new ideas.

For example, a manufacturer of trailers in Newcastle might wish to sell them to the end-customer himself (perhaps, in order to avoid losing a large share of the retail price to middlemen). But manufacturing and retailing are essentially two separate businesses. People in Devon are unlikely to travel to Newcastle to buy a trailer, when there is probably a supplier of a range of comparable trailers already based in their own area. Even if the Newcastle manufacturer sets up a shop in Devon, people may still be inclined to visit other retailers who offer a wider range of choice, or have local contacts. More sales will be achieved by sticking firmly to the core activity of manufacturing, and developing a distribution network through dealers around the country.

In time, your business may have the resources to expand its operation and become something else, but, initially, if you try to start two businesses, you will have to generate the cash flow and return for two businesses, which is (at least) twice as difficult as generating them for one.

Where Is Your Market?

Starting out, you are unlikely to be able to tackle the whole market for your product or service. You will instead look for a suitable segment of that market. That might be defined geographically – the North West, Manchester, even a particular housing estate.

Alternatively, your segment might be defined as a product niche. For example, specialised stopwatches for use in sports, but not all sorts of watches or clocks.

However, even though you may decide only to tackle a small part of a market, you cannot afford to ignore what is happening in the whole market. For example, if you are opening the first small corner-shop on a new housing estate, you should foresee that any one of several supermarket chains might open a shop nearby and become your main competition. Perhaps you could overcome this by becoming a franchisee of one of the chains yourself.

On the other hand, if your product will be manufactured and sold locally, for instance, in Manchester, but must compete against products from international suppliers, you have to monitor what is going on in the international field as well as in the national market.

You need to look beyond your immediate market to see what the longer-term trends are:

- Is the size of your market growing or declining?

- Is it characterised by rapid innovation or evolution of products?

- Is it expanding geographically (as might be the case with an innovative product/service)?

- Is the number of competitors expanding or declining?

- Are prices rising or falling?

You need to end up with figures that show the size and growth potential of the total market – but these must be made relevant to your business proposal, in terms of the part of the market (the market segment) that you are targeting.

These concepts will help you to define your market:

- Wholesale or retail?

- One product or a range of products?

- A product or a service?

- A necessity or a luxury?

If your idea is very innovative and no market yet exists for it, it may be difficult to define what your market is likely to be. Obtaining hard information about the size and value of your market may be daunting. However, you must be able to provide this information in your business plan because it is a key element in establishing the existence of a market for your product and the cost structure that your business must attain in order to be competitive.

If you get this information wrong, other assumptions are likely to be invalid and your project may fail, perhaps at considerable loss to yourself. Equally, if bankers and other investors cannot find independent verification for the figures in your proposal, they will certainly have doubts regarding its overall viability, and are likely to refuse to finance you.

Who Are Your Customers?

You must build as accurate a profile of your customers as you can. This depends on the type of business you plan to run.

For a corner-shop, the customers will be diverse in age, gender and requirements: everyone from children wanting sweets for a few pennies to adults wanting newspapers, grocery items and perhaps small gift items. On the other hand, an information technology company producing a single product, say an automated accounting package for bookmakers, has a very narrowly defined customer base.

Some useful questions to ask about your customers are:

- General public or business, or both?

- Public sector or private?

- Where do they live/operate?

- What and how much do they buy, at what price, when and why?

- What age are they?

- What gender?

- Are they spending for a necessity or a luxury; in other words, do they buy out of surplus income?

- Are they rich or poor?

For your product/service, are there criteria that define your customers, such as:

- A particular interest (for example, travel or sport)?

- Need for a particular service (for example, training to use accounting software)?

In terms of business customers, there may be other criteria to consider:

- Size of customer – will you only supply customers taking more than (or less than) a certain volume?

- Quality levels for the product (these may be imposed by certain wholesale purchasers, department/chain stores, etc.)

- Type of packaging preferred.

In considering who your customers are, you may also need to consider how easy it will be to deal with them. Larger organisations will have more decision-makers than small ones, and it may take longer to negotiate contracts and persuade them to take your product – although the resulting orders are likely to be bigger. To deal with the public sector, it is necessary to understand how it is structured, how decisions are made and who makes them.

Will your business deal only with one segment of the market, such as the public sector, or will you be tackling several segments? How much experience do you have in dealing with each segment? Do you have the resources to service more than one segment? Will you deal with them on the same terms? And, if not, how will you prevent sales 'leaking' to the segment that gets the most favourable terms?

Who Is Your Competition?

Look hard at your own product/service. How does it differ from competing products/services? Very few businesses are genuinely innovative; most compete with existing businesses.

So, why should a customer prefer your product/service?

- Better quality?

- Lower price?

- Higher profile?

What do your sales depend on?

- Price?

- Design?

- Advertising?

- Quality?
- Volume?
- After-sales service?
- Speed of delivery?
- Accessibility?

An important question is whether your product/service's differentiating feature is the one that makes the customer prefer it. Take the examples of a perfume or a luxury car. It would be pointless to make cheaper versions of either, since buyers value the image that the high price gives. Exclusive products are characterised by low-volume/high-margin sales. Their success depends on high marketing expenditure and careful selection and monitoring of distribution outlets.

If, on the other hand, your product/service's sale is characterised by high volumes and low margins, such as margarine or flour or fast food, your business needs to be structured very differently, with more emphasis on volume production, warehousing, constancy of supply and a good distribution network.

When looking at your competition, you may need to consider products/services that compete indirectly with yours, as well as those that compete directly. For example, if you produce frozen hamburgers, you compete not only against other frozen hamburger manufacturers, but against a variety of other cheap frozen food products, including fish fingers, vegetable burgers, pies and so on.

You need to find out:

- How many other companies supply products/services similar to yours?
- How will they react to your entry to the market place?
- Are all the companies in the market place the same size?
- Are they very much bigger than you?

- Have you the resources to equal their power in the market?

- Do new entrants normally start small and grow, or will you have to make a major commitment from the start?

Price

The next piece of market information that you should research is the price that the market will pay for your product/service. How much will customers pay? Under what circumstances will they pay more?

You will generally be constrained by the market. You cannot charge more than the going price for your product/service unless it has something special to recommend it. Even then, a large number of customers may still choose the lower-priced option.

Forecasting Sales

If you thought the earlier elements of your market research were hard, forecasting sales makes them look like child's play.

Despite the difficulty, you need to have a good idea of likely sales (with some evidence to underpin your figures) in order to:

- Build your financial projections

- Estimate the production capacity you require

- Arrange for supply of materials

- Hire staff.

Your requirements on each of these will vary depending on the sales volumes and values that you expect.

Start with a clean sheet of paper. Draw columns for each month and deep rows for each product or service (or variant thereof) that you expect to sell. Within each row, list the promotional and other activity that you plan to use to generate sales. (If you haven't planned any yet, it's time to start – products don't just sell on their own, they usually have to be sold). Then, make some estimates month by month of the sales that will result from this activity. You may find it easier to forecast unit sales first and then to estimate sales value.

For example, if you intend to design and sell Mother's Day greetings cards, it's likely that most of your sales will happen in March – with perhaps a few early orders in February – but none after that, until the next year. So, in this case, your sales forecast exercise should naturally lead you into new product development – cards for Father's Day or Hallowe'en and so on.

It's important to break down sales to the lowest level of product/service that you can manage without overwhelming yourself in detail.

Where you can, get forward orders or 'letters of comfort' from customers. These are better evidence in support of your forecasts than any market research – although your market research is still essential.

Calculating Costs and Profit Margins

As part of your business planning (see **Chapter 4**), you will prepare financial projections for inclusion in your business plan.

However, at this stage, it is a good idea to estimate (even crudely) the minimum size or capacity at which you will make a profit – the break-even point – as well as the maximum operating capacity that you can afford to establish. To do this, you will need to work out what your costs of production will be – you already know the price the market will pay for your product, and how many units you expect to be able to sell.

You also need to identify the current market profit margins – how much your competitors are making. You may be prepared to accept a slimmer margin, but this may reduce your flexibility to deal with unexpected demands. It may also shorten the length of time your business can afford to wait to reach the break-even point. If you look for larger than average profit margins, without either reducing costs or convincing customers that your product is worth paying more for, you will quickly find yourself in difficulty.

Will your entry to the market reduce profit margins generally? If you increase the total supply of product available, it may have the effect of reducing the price for which it sells. It may even trigger a price war, as existing suppliers try to kill off your business before it gets going by cutting their prices below the price you must get to stay in business.

Even if you are successful, you will most likely only get a part of the market, not the whole. Yet, if you cannot meet the average costs achieved by your direct competitors, you may fail, even though your product/service may be better than theirs.

The income generated by sales must provide sufficient cash flow to enable your business to cover all costs. If money comes in too slowly, your business can choke to death while demand booms. Cash flow – collecting money from customers as quickly as possible and getting the longest possible credit period from your suppliers – is often more important in the short term for a small business than profit. But, overall, you must make a profit to stay in business.

Estimating Your Initial Investment

At this stage, you should draw up a list of what premises and equipment you absolutely must have (not what it would be nice to have).

How do you know how much you need? Close your eyes and picture yourself running your new business. What do you see? List it all – use the **Start-up Investment** worksheet on the next page to help you.

START-UP INVESTMENT

Investment required	£
Premises (deposit, first month's rent, etc)	
Renovations	
Fixtures and fittings	
Transport	
Machines and equipment	
Goodwill, security deposits	
Miscellaneous	
Initial stock of raw materials	
Expenses paid before start-up	
Other start-up costs	
Contingency	
TOTAL INVESTMENT	

Check that you have not forgotten anything. Then, cross off everything that's not *absolutely* necessary. Note where you already have equipment or materials.

Next, start pricing your list. Think about buying second-hand to save money, where possible. Finally, add a sizeable amount – perhaps 50% or 100% more – as a contingency, to cover things you have not yet thought of.

You need to answer these questions:

- Will it be possible to keep overheads low by working from your garage or a spare room? (What about planning permission from your local authority?)

- Do you need retail premises in a good location?

- What about warehouse space?

- Do you need specialised equipment? How big is it?

- Will you have to make a large capital investment in equipment? Can you lease equipment instead? Can you buy it second-hand?

From this information, and from your other market research, you will be able to estimate your start-up investment – what you need to get started.

Finding the Best Business Structure

Lastly, you need to decide what form your business organisation should take. When starting in business, you have a choice of business entity through which to conduct your enterprise:

- Sole trader

- Partnership

- Limited liability partnership

- Limited liability company.

Four things will decide which you choose:

- The kind of business you are starting: Some professional firms, for instance, are usually formed as sole traders or partnerships.

- The expectations of those with whom you plan to do business: Many business people expect to deal with limited liability companies and are wary of other forms of business entities as trading partners.

- Your attitude to risk: In particular, to risking those of your assets that you are not planning to commit to the business. A limited liability company limits the risk of losing your capital if your enterprise is not successful.

- How you wish to organise your tax affairs: Different tax rules apply to different types of business structure.

You are taking a risk in starting an enterprise. You are risking your money, time and reputation. You are entitled to protect those of your assets that you do not wish to commit to your enterprise. For this reason, and for your family's sake, you are strongly advised to form a limited liability company (although it may not be essential starting out). You ought to take the professional advice of your accountants in making your decision. If you do not yet have an accountant, read the section *Choosing an Accountant* in **Chapter 10**.

Next, consider how your business will be organised internally. The main functional areas in any business are:

- Administration

- Marketing

- Sales

- Production

- Distribution.

What should be the balance between these functions within your company? (Note that Production follows after Marketing and Sales – keep this order of priority firmly in your mind at all times – too many entrepreneurs try to sell what they can make, it's better to try to make, or buy in, what the customer wants to buy!).

Among the questions you need to ask yourself are:

- How will you get your product to the customer?

- Will you need large amounts of warehouse space?

- What are your costs of production?

- What are the overheads involved?

SOURCES OF INFORMATION

There is no shortage of information available to help you in your market research – most entrepreneurs starting out find that their main problem is too much information!

Consider all of these sources:

- Yourself

- Professional advisers

- Trade and professional associations

- Libraries

- Telephone directories

- Other people

- Government and private sector enterprise support agencies

- Professional researchers

- The Internet.

Yourself

Most people will have started to research their idea long before they come to the formal planning stage. Often, the idea has grown out of a long period of personal interest and their initial research is based on:

- Personal experience

- Talking to friends

- Talking to suppliers.

Many good business ideas provide an answer to a problem with existing products. If you have an idea for a new type of light fitting, it is probably because over the years you have become exasperated by the failings of the many light fittings that you have used. So, immediately, you know what advantage your potential product offers above others in the market.

You may have to find out about the costs of making it, how it can/should be distributed and who your competitors are before you can make an estimate of the size of the market and, most importantly, whether it is feasible financially to be a small manufacturer of light fittings only. You might discover that the machinery required is so expensive that you would have to make and sell a huge number of fittings – or adapt to making and selling other items also – in order to pay for it.

Professional Advisers

Bank managers and accountants often have a good idea of how different types of businesses are faring, and what differentiates the successes from those that cannot pay the bills. Also, talking to your bank manager like this is a gentle introduction to your idea of starting your own business.

Banks usually have specialists in a variety of industry sectors, who can be useful sources of market information and statistics. Approach your bank manager or the small business lending unit of your bank as a first step. They may be able to find the information for you, or direct you to someone who can.

Trade and Professional Associations

If a trade or professional association exists for the market sector in which you are interested, it may be an excellent source of information about the total size and value of your market. It may even have statistics broken down by region.

Some associations may only make this information available to members – and, if you are not yet in business, you may find it difficult to gain access to it. Other associations will make the information publicly available, though there is usually a charge involved as the organisation tries to recover some of its own costs.

Many associations have links to sister bodies internationally and thus can be a source of international statistics and information. Most of these organisations provide training, networking and other services to their members so, if an association is relevant to your business, it's worth considering joining at the earliest possible opportunity.

Libraries

Often overlooked, local libraries have a wealth of information available – either on the spot or available through inter-library loans. Make a friend of your local librarian – he or she has valuable research skills that you will spend a great deal of time to acquire yourself.

Bigger cities often have a dedicated business library – those in London and Belfast are particularly good.

And, increasingly, libraries provide access to the Internet (see next page) for a modest charge.

Telephone Directories

Classified telephone directories are a useful guide to the number of people doing what you want to do and their location.

You want to be a carpenter? Look up carpenters in the phone book. If there are 15 in your locality, either it is a great place for carpenters or they are all very poor!

Other People in the Business

Talk to people already involved in the industry. Make use of their experience. Trade and professional associations may be able to put you in contact with some of their members who may be willing to share their experience and expertise.

If yours is (or will be) a technology business, identify a 'Centre of Excellence' in your field. *Universities* have a wealth of information and experience at their disposal, much of which is available – usually, for a fee.

Government and Private Sector Enterprise Support Agencies

There is a vast range of support available to entrepreneurs and those thinking of starting a business. Much of it is provided by Government or Government-funded agencies; some of it is provided by the private sector.

Professional Researchers

If the market for your product is geographically extensive, or highly competitive, you might consider getting professional market researchers to prepare a report for you. Look in a classified telephone directory for contact details of market researchers in your area.

The Internet

Another source of information – particularly on international trends – is the Internet. If you are not already connected to the Internet, ask a friend to show you or visit your local library or a cybercafé where you can rent access by the hour.

Use one of the search engines – Yahoo, Lycos, Alta Vista, etc. – to help narrow your enquiries. Contact the companies whose websites you visit for more information.

There is a huge range of websites aimed at start-ups.

Summary

Chapters 5, 6, 7 and **8** give details of support for entrepreneurs and small business in England, Scotland, Wales and Northern Ireland respectively, while **Chapter 9** provides information on EU support.

In addition, the **Directory of Sources of Support** provides contact details for all organisations mentioned in this book. The companion website, **www.startingabusinessinbritain.com**, will keep you up to date on any changes.

INTERPRETING RESEARCH RESULTS

Researching your proposed business is not just a matter of asking the right questions. Interpreting the results is equally important. You may be too close to your idea to see problems (or, less often, to see opportunities). Bringing in outsiders may be helpful. Consider friends whose business skills you respect. Ask your accountant, banker or other professional adviser – even if you have to pay for their opinion. It is important to arrive at an independently objective point of view, and it will be worth paying for if it saves you from disaster.

In addition to giving an independent view of your plans, a good accountant can help you draw up financial projections. In any case, you will probably need an accountant once you have begun trading. An accountant who is introduced at the planning stage will have a greater insight into the objectives of the business as well as the systems by which it functions. Your planning will benefit from the experience of your accountant, who, in turn, will be better placed to give you good service in future years.

THE FINAL QUESTION

Now you are in a position to answer the question at the start of this chapter: Does a market for your product or service exist? Your answer will tell you whether to proceed to the next stage.

If not, don't despair. It's better to have found out that your idea won't work before you have invested much time and effort into it – and, if you're serious about starting your own business, there'll be plenty of other opportunities.

3

WRITING A BUSINESS PLAN

Once you have done thoroughly the necessary market research for your project and decided to go ahead and start your own business, your next step is to write a business plan that summarises the following points about your business:

- Where it has come from

- Where it is now

- Where it is going in the future

- How it intends to get there

- How much money it needs to fulfil its plans

- What makes it likely to succeed

- What threats or disadvantages must be overcome on the way.

A business plan can range in length from a few typed sheets of paper to several hundred pages. However, since professional readers of business plans – bankers, venture capitalists and enterprise advisers – are offered more business plans than they can intelligently digest, the more concise your business plan, the more likely it is to be read.

THE PURPOSE OF A BUSINESS PLAN

A business plan can have several purposes. The main ones usually are:

- To establish the fundamental viability of your project
- To document your plan for the business
- To act as a yardstick for measuring progress against plans
- To communicate your plans for your business to outsiders, particularly those you want to invest in your business.

Although the business plan is most often used as a marketing document for raising finance, even if you do not need to raise finance you should still prepare one since it will:

- Focus your thoughts
- Check your numbers
- Provide a basis for monitoring results
- Enable communication of your ideas.

Each of these purposes places its own demands on the format and contents of the business plan.

The focus of your business plan will vary, depending on the relative priorities that you assign to these purposes. Let's look at each in turn.

Establishing the Viability of Your Project

There are many ways of researching whether your project will succeed. All, however, finally require an act of faith from the entrepreneur when the time comes to commit to the business. Before this point is reached, a great deal of planning and careful thought should have been completed.

A well-prepared business plan will assist immeasurably with that process, simply through the discipline it imposes. Too often, entrepreneurs are carried away with their own enthusiasm. They neglect the most cursory checks on the viability of their brainchild. Broad, and sometimes rash, assumptions are made about the market for the product, its cost of manufacture, distribution channels, acceptability to customers, etc. But when a reasoned, written case must be made – even if only to oneself – it is less easy to overlook the unpalatable. At least, it is difficult to do so without being aware of it.

Documenting the Plan

'The plan doesn't matter, it's the planning that counts', said Dwight D. Eisenhower, former US President. He was right. The quality of the planning you do for your business is critical to its success; how you document that planning process is less so. Nonetheless, a good business plan actively aids the planning process by providing a structure. It forces you:

- To cover ground that you might otherwise, in your enthusiasm, skip over

- To clarify your thinking — it is almost impossible to get your plan onto paper until you have formulated it clearly

- To justify your arguments, since they will be written down for all to see

- To focus on the risks and potential for loss in your plans as well as on the potential for profit and success.

Avoid unnecessary pessimism. Be realistic, but don't carry caution to extremes. If your proposal is realistic, have confidence in it.

A Yardstick for Measuring Progress

Preparing any plan demands an objective. An objective assumes that you are going to make some effort to achieve it. Some objectives are quantifiable: if your aim is to sell 500 gadgets, sales of 480 is below target, while 550 units sold gives you reason to feel pleased with your performance. Other objectives cannot be quantified; all the more reason then to document them so that you can more easily establish whether or not you have achieved them.

Your business plan should contain the objectives, quantifiable and otherwise, that you have set for your business. Reading through your plan at regular intervals and comparing your performance to date with the objectives that you set yourself one month, six months or two years earlier can help to focus your attention on the important things that need to be done if those targets are to be achieved.

Communicating Plans to Third Parties

Though they would readily acknowledge the importance of good planning, many business-owners would not prepare a formal business plan if it were not for the need to present their plans for the business to outsiders – usually to raise finance. Too often, the urgent pushes aside the important. But, if you wish to raise finance for your business to develop, you will have to prepare a business plan.

Financiers, whether bankers, venture capitalists or private investors, need:

- A document they can study in their own time, and which makes its case independently of the promoters of the business

- Evidence that the future of the business has been properly planned and that all risks have been taken into account

- Information about the business.

In addition, others may have reason to read your business plan – key employees or suppliers, for example. So it must communicate your message clearly.

No matter how good a writer you consider yourself to be, if you can't put your business proposition clearly and persuasively in writing, it suggests that you have more thinking to do. It doesn't mean that your project won't work. On the contrary, your business may be a resounding success – but you need to be able to communicate it!

WHO SHOULD WRITE YOUR BUSINESS PLAN?

Very simply, you. No one else.

You may receive offers from consultants, many of them highly reputable and professional in their work, to write your business plan for you. They will quote their extensive experience of business, of raising finance for start-up businesses, of presenting financial information – all valid points and, in many cases, true.

However, whatever experience consultants may have of business in general, and drafting business plans in particular, they lack one essential ingredient: your intimate relationship with your business. You are the one who has spent your waking hours – and many of your sleeping ones, too, probably – dreaming, planning and guiding your tender and frail creation to this point. You know what makes you tick; what makes your team tick; what will and will not work for you. Only you can assemble these thoughts.

Therefore, the first draft of the business plan is your responsibility – and yours alone. Do it yourself. Refine and redraft it – again, and again, if necessary – until it's finished.

Then, and only then, should you entrust it to someone who can put the right gloss on it. But let them do only that. Don't let them put *their* words on your pages.

HOW LONG SHOULD YOUR BUSINESS PLAN BE?

How long is a piece of string? Your business plan should be as long as it needs to be – no longer and no shorter.

How long is that? No one can decide that except yourself. It depends on the purpose for which you are preparing the plan, the level of knowledge that likely readers will have of your business, and the complexity of your business.

Few businesses can be done justice to in less than a half-dozen A4 pages; equally, it will be a dedicated reader (or one who has spotted an outstandingly good business proposition) who will continue past the first hundred pages or so.

If a reader wants more information, they will ask for it. But make sure that they don't have to ask for information they should have had from the start – or, worse still (and sometimes fatal to your hopes of raising finance), that the absence of essential information doesn't lead them to discard your plan altogether.

FIGURES

Too many figures and your plan may become off-putting, but too few and your plans will simply be treated as ambitions without any underlying substance. Quantify as much as you can. Your plan is likely to be read by people whose currency is numbers. You help your cause by talking their language.

Make sure figures add up correctly. Nothing is more worrying to an investor than the suspicion that:

- You can't handle figures

- There's a figure wrong or missing – or worse still, hidden.

You need to be able to show the existence of a market for your product, and some indication of its size, in a way that can be verified independently. You will also have to prove to the satisfaction of the bank manager or investor that adequate margins can be achieved to cover cash flow needs and meet repayment of debt or growth objectives.

Don't clog up the body of the business plan with detailed statistical analysis, although it must contain all the information a reader needs. For example, quote the proposed sales target, but show how you will achieve it in an Appendix, and explain the underlying assumptions there also. The same applies to the CVs of key employees – mention crucial information where appropriate in the plan, but place the details in an Appendix.

Business Models and Projected Figures

A financial model of the business is effectively a set of accounts, represented on computer spreadsheets or in a dedicated modelling package for ease of manipulation – for example, from *Business Plan Pro* from Palo Alto Software.

While a financial model is useful for businesses of all sizes, for a business of any complexity it is essential. Your model should enable you to change certain variables, such as the number of units of product sold, or the price at which you sell them, or the cost of supplies, and discover what the effect will be on the business.

Your financial model should consist of:

- Balance sheet

- Profit and loss account

- Cash flow statement.

You may also create some management accounts that look in more detail at production and overhead costs and allow you to manipulate certain of those variables – but only if your business needs this level of sophistication. Don't complicate things!

It is crucial that the figures you use in your model are as close to reality as can be. Your model must show what your breakeven point is likely to be in different circumstances, and allow you to estimate how long it will take to reach it. This calculation is very important when it comes to raising finance. If you will be able to repay borrowings in three to six months, you may be willing to risk a bigger initial loan than if your earliest estimated repayment date is a year or two away.

The rule is to be cautious and prudent, but realistic. If your figures are too optimistic, you could find that you cannot meet your repayment schedule, and the additional cost of borrowing over a longer time frame damages your growth prospects, if not your viability – and your credibility with your bank manager. Equally, if you are unnecessarily pessimistic about the length of time it will take to repay the loan, your calculations may indicate that the entire project should be dropped – which is exactly what your bank manager will do!

Some of the main reasons for using a financial model are to estimate:

- A breakeven point under different market conditions

- How long it will take to reach a desired level of operation

- The consequences of price changes

- The consequences of undertaking expansion, R&D, and other special projects.

Again, the details of the assumptions on which the model is based should go into an Appendix to the business plan, as should any detailed statistical analysis. Quote the important final figures in the body of the plan.

A STANDARD BUSINESS PLAN FORMAT

Each business plan is unique. However, those whom you seek to convince to invest in your project have come to expect certain information in a broadly standard format that presents information in an easily digested and logical sequence.

For a very small or simple business, the simple and intuitive format on the next page (adapted from *Applying the Rules of Business*, Ron Immink & Brian O'Kane, Oak Tree Press, ISBN 1-86076-275-1) may be sufficient. Although unorthodox, it covers all the information that a reader of a business plan – and, more importantly, the entrepreneur him/herself – needs to know about the business.

For larger businesses, the format on the page following, adapted from *Planning for Success* (Ron Immink & Brian O'Kane, Oak Tree Press, ISBN 1-872853-89-7) may be more appropriate.

It uses a broadly standard structure of:

1. Summary/Overview

2. The Entrepreneur

3. Formal Requirements

4. Marketing

5. Investments and Financing

6. The Operating Budget

7. Personal Expenses

8. Cash Flow

9. Other Information (included as an Appendix).

In each subsection, it asks a number of questions – you should ensure that the answers to all these questions (or as many as are appropriate to your business) are included in your business plan.

SIMPLE BUSINESS PLAN OUTLINE

I am ...	Explain who you are, your education/work experience etc, especially insofar as it applies to your proposed business.
My product is ...	Explain your product: What it is, what is does, how it works, how it is made, what makes it different/unique, etc.
My customers are ...	Explain who your customers will be and what evidence you have to support this.
My customers will buy my product because ...	Explain why your customers will buy your product and what evidence you have to support this.
My customers will pay ...	Explain how much your customers will pay for each unit of your product and what evidence you have to support this.
At this price, my customers will buy ...	Explain how many units of your product your customers will buy at the price set and what evidence you have to support this.
I can make ...	Explain how many units of your product you can make in a given time period and what evidence you have to support this.
To make each unit of product costs ...	Explain how much each unit of product costs you to make and what evidence you have to support this.
The start-up investment I require is ...	Explain the start-up investment you need, what it will be used for and what evidence you have to support this.
I have a viable business because ...	Explain why you believe you have a viable business and what evidence you have to support this.
In summary ...	On a single page, list the main points of your plan, in bullet point form. This is the part of the business plan that will make the biggest impression on your reader – make sure it's easy to read and understand. Then put it at the front of your plan, where it will be seen!

PLANNING FOR SUCCESS BUSINESS PLAN OUTLINE

1: Summary/Overview

- **Founder(s)**
- **Business name**
- **Contact details:** Address, Telephone/Fax, E-mail, Website.
- **Status:** Sole trader, partnership or limited company/partnership.
- **Registered for:** VAT, PAYE, Corporation Tax.
- **Formed as:** Purchase of existing business/purchase of franchise/start-up/other.
- **Business Objective**
- **External Accountant:** Address, telephone/fax number, contact name.
- **Product/Service Range:** Include descriptions and prices.
- **Staff:** Numbers employed in production, sales/promotion, administration, other duties.
- **Competitors:** Include estimates of competitors' turnover.
- **Investment and Financing:** Details of fixed assets, personal assets, current assets, long/medium-term assets, liquid assets, short-term finance, start-up costs, subsidies/grants, allowance for contingencies, total investment, total available finance.
- **Budgets:** Forecasts for turnover, gross profit, gross profit percentage, net profit, cash flow and personal expenses over first three years.
- **Other Information**.

2: The Entrepreneur
(If there is more than one founder, each must complete this section.)

- **Personal details:** Name, address, date of birth, etc.
- **Income:** Details of present income, source of income, benefits, income of spouse/partner, etc.
- **Education:** Details of post-primary education, including any courses that you are currently attending.
- **Practical Experience:** Details of your working history and experience and any other significant experience that could be useful for your business.
- **Motivation, Objectives and Goals:** Why do you want to start a business? What do you want to achieve with your business?

- **Personal Qualities**: What special qualities of yours are important for your business? List both your strong points and your weak points. What are you going to do about your weak points?

3: Formal Requirements

- **Overall Description**: Give a general description of your proposed business.
- **Research**: List the organisations you have contacted to discuss your plans and summarise the outcome of these discussions.
- **Legal Status**: What legal status will your business take? What considerations led you to this choice?
- **Name and Location**: What is the name of the business? Have you checked that this name is available? Describe your location. How can customers reach your location? Is access for supply and removal of goods available? Is there enough parking for your customers' cars and for your own cars? How big are your office premises? Are there expansion possibilities at these premises? Are the premises leased or purchased? Give details of cost of lease/mortgage. Have the premises been professionally valued? Has a lease or purchase contract been prepared by a solicitor? (If so, give the name of the solicitor.) Is there any pollution in the ground at your premises?
- **Licences**: Do you fulfil all of the licensing and permit requirements for the field you will be working in? If so, which and on what grounds? If not, why not and what are you doing about it? Is your business registered at Companies House (if appropriate)? What other licences do you need? Are there any other legal applications required (for example, environmental concerns). If so, which?
- **Employer and Employees**: Initially, how will your staffing be organised? Have you drawn up clear job descriptions for your future employees? Do you plan to expand your employee numbers quickly? Who will replace you during any required absences?
- **Administration**: Who will do your accounting? Who will do your bookkeeping? Give names, addresses and contact numbers.
- **Insurance**: Are you insured against the normal risks of business? If so, what is insured and for how much?

- **Terms of Trade**: How is responsibility for product delivery arranged? Are product deliveries insured? If so, for how much? Summarise your terms of trade.
- **VAT**: Is your business registered for VAT? What is your VAT number? What rates of VAT apply to your business?
- **Start Date**: On what date do you want to start the business, or when did you start?

4: Marketing

- **Market**: Who are your target groups? What do you have to offer? What is your business objective in seven words?
- **Market Research**: Describe your market, future developments and your potential customers (local, county, national, and international). Describe the level of competition you face. What are the leading indicators in your market sector? Estimate the size of the UK market for your product. What part of this market do you intend to service? Have you contacted future customers? What was their reaction? Have you obtained any forward orders? What comments did you receive with these orders?
- **Image**: What image will your business present? Formulate the core of your marketing plan based on your target groups, product assortment, price level, etc.
- **Product (Range)**: Describe briefly the product(s) you want to launch. Describe the primary and secondary functions of your product(s). What choices do you offer your customers? What extras do you offer compared to the competition?
- **Price**: What are customers prepared to pay? What are customers accustomed to paying? What are your competitors' prices? What is your price? How is your price made up? Will you offer discounts? If so, what will they be? Will you make special offers? If so, what will they be? Will cost calculations be monitored during operation? If so, how?
- **Place**: Explain your choice of location. Are there future developments that will change the attractiveness of your location? How did you allocate space for the various necessary functions?
- **Personnel**: Profile yourself as a businessperson. How many people will be involved in production, sales/promotion, administration, other duties? How are you going to make sure that your staff uphold the image of your business?

- **Presentation**: How are you going to present your business (layout, colours, music, atmosphere, correspondence, brochures, business cards, van signs)?
- **Promotion**: Rate those areas your customers are most interested in, and your relative strengths in those areas. How are you going to approach your customers and what buying motives are you going to emphasise? What marketing and promotion resources will you emphasise? Explain your promotion methods (how, where, frequency, etc.)
- **Competitors**: List your main competitors. Assess their strengths compared to your own. In what ways do your products/services differ from those of your competitors? Can you estimate the total turnover of your competitors? What are your strong points compared to those of your direct competitors? What are your weak points compared to those of your direct competitors?
- **Purchasing**: Have you contacted your future suppliers? If so, what are their terms of trade? Are there alternative suppliers? What advantages do these alternative suppliers offer you?
- **Production Process**: Are you involved with (or will you be using) new techniques or new products in your production processes? If so, are you receiving assistance from experts? If so, who are they and how are they involved? Describe your production process. What experience do you have with this process? What equipment do you use in the production process? List the equipment you intend to lease, buy new, or buy used. What guarantees/back-up do you have for this equipment in case of malfunction? Have you enough capacity to achieve the revenue for which you have budgeted? Have you checked your products and production processes for environmental considerations? If so, are there any environmental objections? If so, what are you planning to do about them?

5: Investment and Financing

- **Investment**: Describe the investment you will have to make to start your business, and to run it over the first three years (amounts exclusive of VAT).
- **Personal Assets**: What assets can you (and your business partner(s), if any) put up yourselves? How did you value your personal assets?
- **Other (Bank) Finance**: Details of long/medium-term finance, short-term finance, subsidies/grants; shortfall, surplus etc.

- **Credit Assessment**: Can you support the required investment in fixed assets with quotations from suppliers? If not, how did you calculate your investment? Is your investment cost-effective? In your estimates, did you take seasonal business influences into account, and calculate based on your maximum requirements? How did you estimate your stock and work-in-progress levels? How did you estimate the value of your debtors? Do you have sufficient liquid assets to cope with disappointments and unexpected expenses? Did you approach a bank (or banks) about the financing of your plans? If yes, which bank(s), and who was your contact person? Did those contacts lead to any agreements? Did you approach other finance companies about your plans? If yes, with whom did you speak? Were any decisions reached, or arrangements made?

6: The Operating Budget

- **Turnover Forecast**: List your revenue sources, and project the amounts you expect from each in the first three years.
- **Costs**: Give details of costs for staff, production, premises, transport, sales and promotion, general expenses, finance and depreciation in each of the first three years.
- **Profits and Cash Flow**: Give detailed cash-flow projections for the first three years.
- **Comments on the Budget**: Describe how you calculated and estimated your revenue (number of customers, average order per customer, turnaround). What expansion do you expect over the next few years? How did you calculate your purchase costs? How did you estimate salaries? What effect will any shortfall in turnover have on your business and how do you plan to handle it? What is your minimum required turnover?

7: Personal Expenses

- **Personal Expenses**: Fixed expenses; rent/mortgage repayment; gas, water, electricity; local taxes/charges; insurance; study expenses; membership expenses/contributions; TV licence; private use of car; loan repayments (enclose loan details); household expenses, etc.
- **Home Equity**: Do you own your own home? If so, have you had it valued? What is its market value? How much equity do you have in your house?

- **Additional Debts**: What other debts do you have (personal/ private loan or credit, car financing, study costs, etc.)?
- **Minimum Required Turnover**: What is the minimum required turnover for your business, including your personal expenses?

8: Cash Flow

- Detailed cash-flow projections for each month of each quarter, outlining all income and expenditure, together with the opening and closing bank balances each quarter over the first three years.

Sometimes the Summary/Overview at the start of the business plan is expanded with a narrative Executive Summary, a concise one- or two-page summary of the entire plan.

The last section of a business plan to be written, and the first to be read, an Executive Summary must persuade the reader that the idea is good, otherwise he or she may not read on. It summarises the company, its objectives, and why it will be successful. It describes the products, the market, critical financial information and, finally, outlines what form of finance is required, how much, and when. It assumes that its reader is not expert in your industry and knows nothing about your business. And it does all this in as few words as possible!

You should avoid giving detailed personal reasons in your business plan for wanting to be your own boss. It is very easy to confuse your personal ambitions with your objectives for the business. Bankers and other investors are primarily interested in your prospects for success (and, as a consequence, a good return on their investment), not your prospects for personal satisfaction. It is important to keep your focus, like theirs, on the business. Your character and skills will be of importance to them; these are the things to mention.

HOW A FINANCIER READS A BUSINESS PLAN

How a financier reads a business plan depends on what kind of financier he, or increasingly she, is. There are two types of financier – the lender and the investor.

The lender is typically your bank manager. Lenders will invest money in your business, if they think it worth doing so by their criteria, in return for interest on the capital. The professional investor, on the other hand, will invest equity in your business and share in your risk as part-owner of the business. Professional investors will postpone their return for a period – typically, three to five years – but will look for an above-average return for the risk involved in doing so.

The Lender

The average bank manager will be looking to see how you propose to handle the risks, particularly the financial risks, that your business is likely to encounter. Bank managers are concerned about the security of the bank's money – or more properly, the depositors' money – which you are seeking and for which they are responsible.

That is not to say that a bank manager will not back you. Most bank managers have some discretion in the amounts they lend to businesses and will sometimes back their own hunches or gut feelings against the apparent odds. But do not bet on it. Turn the odds in your favour by writing your business plan and framing your request for finance in the best possible light.

Arnold S. Goldstein, American author of *Starting on a Shoestring* (John Wiley & Sons, ISBN 0-471-13415-5), suggests the following likely line of questioning from a bank manager:

- Why do you need the amount requested?

- What will you do with it?

- How do you know it's enough?

- How much less can you live with?

- Who else will you borrow from?

- How do you propose to repay it?

- How can you prove that you can?

- What collateral can you offer?

Unless you can answer these questions to your bank manager's satisfaction, it is unlikely that you will get the money you are looking for.

And don't wait for the interview with the manager for an opportunity to give the answers to these questions – that is far too late. The bank manager's mind will already be made up, more or less, before your meeting. Your plan will have been read thoroughly. The interview is intended to firm up the manager's decision. If you have not answered the relevant questions in the plan, you are not likely to have much chance to do so later.

You don't need to write your business plan in a style that asks the questions in the form above and then gives the answers. What you need to do is to ensure that the information that answers the questions is:

- Contained within the plan

- Visible within the plan

- Capable of being extracted easily by a reader from the plan.

Putting all this in another way, a bank manager will look for three things:

- Character

- Collateral

- Cash flow.

Character means you. A bank manager who has any reason to distrust or disbelieve you – from previous dealings or because of your reputation or because of errors or inconsistencies in your business plan – will not invest money with you.

Collateral means the backing that you can give as security for the loan. In some cases, collateral is not needed. But to the banker, who is responsible to the bank's depositors for their money, security is all. If you can offer collateral, it will certainly help your case.

Cash flow means your ability to repay the loan on time, out of the proceeds of the investment. The bank manager will prefer to see the loan repaid at regular monthly or quarterly intervals with interest paid on the due dates – anything else upsets the system. Unless you can show that the business will generate enough cash to make the payments the bank manager requires – or you have explained clearly in your business plan why this will not be possible for an initial period – you will not get the money that you ask for.

Professional Investors

Professional investors, venture capitalists for example, have a different viewpoint. They accept risk, though, like any prudent investor, they will avoid undue risk and seek to limit their exposure to unavoidable risk. David Silver, another American venture capitalist and author on enterprise, suggests that their questions will be along the lines of:

- How much can I make?

- How much can I lose?

- How do I get my money out?

- Who says this is any good?

- Who else is in it?

How much can I make? decides whether the project fits the profile of 30 to 50 per cent annual compound growth (well in excess of bank interest) usually required by such investors.

How much can I lose? identifies the downside risk. Although venture capitalists are used to investing in 10 projects for every one that succeeds, they cannot invest in projects that would jeopardise their own business of investment in the event of their failure.

How do I get my money out? is important since few venture capitalists invest for the long term. Most are happy to turn over their investments every three to five years. None will invest in a project unless they can see clearly an exit mechanism. There is no point in holding a 25 per cent share in a company valued at several million pounds if you cannot realise the shareholding when you want to.

Who says this is any good? Professional investors maintain networks of advisers, often on an informal basis. Venture capitalists will check out all that you say or include in your business plan. This is part of the 'due diligence' process. If you can supply a venture capitalist with evidence that those who ought to know support your plans, you will strengthen your case.

Who else is in this? panders to the investor's residual need for security. Even if investors know that they are going to take a risk, to place their faith and money in your hands, they like to know that others have come to the same conclusion. There is nothing like unanimity to convince people that they are right.

One should not mock – particularly if you're trying to persuade someone to invest. Some venture capitalists have such a reputation for being right, for picking winners, that others try to follow their lead whenever they can.

Above all, in assessing the project itself, a professional investor will look at three key areas:

• **The market:** Is it large and growing rapidly?

- **The product:** Does it solve an important problem in the market?

- **Management:** Are all the key functional areas on board?

WRITING A BUSINESS PLAN

There are three stages in writing a business plan:

- Thinking

- Writing

- Editing.

Each is important but the most important is the first – thinking (which includes market research). Be prepared to spend at least 70 per cent of the time you have allocated to preparing your business plan in thinking. Time spent here will not be wasted. Use this time to talk through your business with anyone who will listen; read widely, especially about others in your area of business; and avoid finding reasons why things cannot be done.

Writing can be done fastest of all – it should probably account for less than half the remaining time available. Use a word processor, if you can. You will need the flexibility it gives to edit the document later.

If you find it difficult to start writing on a blank page or computer screen, talk instead. Buy, or borrow, a hand-held dictating machine. Talk to yourself about your business. Explain it to someone who knows nothing about it. Get the tape transcribed and your business plan will be on the way.

Editing is the last task. Editing is an art. Some people are better at it than others, but everyone can learn the basics. Read through your draft business plan – aloud, if you find that helps. Does what you have written say what you want? Start deleting. You will find that quite a lot can come out without doing damage to the message that you are trying to communicate. When you are happy with your draft, put it aside for a day or two. Come back to it fresh and see whether it still makes sense. Edit again where it does not. And when it is right, leave it alone!

4

FINANCING YOUR START-UP

The 'Golden Rule' for financing a new business is: As little as possible, as cheaply as possible.

Do not put money into the unnecessary. It is better to start off running your business from an attic without a loan than in a glossy, but unnecessary, high street office with heavy bank borrowings.

On the other hand, do adopt a realistic position on the amount of money that you need to get going. Your financing will have to be sufficient to carry the business until it reaches a balance, where money coming in equals money going out – this may take longer than you think (or would like!). In addition to capital investment in plant, equipment and premises, your financing may have to supply most of the working capital until sales begin to generate sufficient income to give you an adequate cash flow.

You have two options in raising finance:

- **Equity:** Capital invested in the business, usually not repayable

- **Debt:** Capital lent to the business, usually repayable at a specified date.

EQUITY

For equity, the alternatives are:

- **Your own equity** – which leads to two questions: How much do you have? How much do you need?

- **Other people's equity** – which also leads to two questions: Are you prepared to allow other people to own part of your business? Can your business offer the sort of return that will attract outside investors?

Owners' Equity

In terms of the equity that you are able to put into the business, you must establish what assets you want to retain as a fallback position, and remove these from the equation. For example, you may not want to mortgage your house to raise finance for your business. Then consider what assets remain in the following terms:

- How easily can they be sold and how much will their sale raise?

- Are they mortgageable assets?

- Will they be acceptable as collateral?

Typical assets include: cash, shares, car(s), land, house(s), boats, second/holiday homes, antiques, jewellery, paintings, etc.

If you are considering mortgaging your family home for the sake of the business, you should be aware that this is a very serious step and professional advice should be obtained. Note that if you mortgage your home, or borrow personally, in order to invest equity into your business, and the business fails, you still remain liable to repay the loan. There's a big difference between this and the situation where the bank lends directly to the business.

Other Equity

For many small businesses, the option of raising equity capital is not a reality. Either the sums they need are too small to interest an investor, or the level of return, while adequate to pay a standard bank loan, is not sufficient to tempt the investor who is exposed to a greater risk. Most equity investors look to invest at least £500,000 in a company, arguing that amounts below this do not justify the amount of checking they need to do before making an investment. Thus, perversely perhaps, it is easier to raise £5,000,000 than it is to raise £50,000.

However, the number of venture capital funds in the UK has increased significantly. Some of these will consider investing seed capital (less than £100,000), although most prefer to invest venture (£100,000 to £500,000, for businesses at an early stage of development) or development (£500,000+) capital. Note that these amounts are arbitrary; some funds will invest in more than one category.

In most cases – certainly where you require seed capital – you can approach the fund manager directly. A check on the fund's website to make sure that you meet the fund's criteria, a phone call to check the name of the person to whom you should send your business plan – then go for it!

Larger, technology-based projects requiring greater and more complex financing can choose whether to go directly to an appropriate fund or to work through a corporate finance house, which has specialist skills in fund-raising.

Whatever your route, remember that it's not just about money, as the growth of incubators (see **Chapter 1**) shows. Depending on the strengths of your new business, supports may be as important as cash.

But, despite all the venture capital funds, the best source of small-scale seed capital for most start-ups continues to be family or friends. If you do decide to involve family and friends as investors in your business, make sure both sides know – and agree on – the ground rules:

- Their investment is 'risk capital' – it may be lost and is not repayable (unless you specifically agree otherwise)

- Equity investment does not automatically give a right to management involvement – even if it is clear that you cannot cope

- Their investment may be diluted by other later investors, whose money is needed to continue the development of the business.

Put everything in writing – in a formal shareholders' agreement, if appropriate, or a simple letter of understanding signed by all parties.

'Business Angels', a term adapted from the world of theatre where private investors ('angels') are often the source of finance for a new show on New York's Broadway or in London's West End, are private investors who take (usually) a minority stake in a business – sometimes with an active management role, too. They're hard to find and, since they're usually experienced business-people, often hard to convince. But a good business angel (there are few bad ones, because they don't last long!) can add far more than just the money they bring. Their contacts, general business sense and experience all can make a significant difference to the growth of your business.

Because equity means giving away part of your business, it's in your interest to minimise the amount held by outside investors. However, be sensible – it's better to own 70% of a thriving and profitable business than 100% of a business going nowhere because it is starved for funds.

DEBT

When considering financing your business with debt, you must consider:

- Fixed or floating
- Long-term or short-term.

Fixed debt is a loan that is secured on a specific asset, for example, on premises. Floating debt is secured on assets that change regularly, for example, debtors. 'Secured' means that, in the event that the loan is not repaid, the lender can appoint a receiver to sell the asset on which the loan is secured in order to recover the amount due. Thus, giving security for a loan is not something to be done lightly.

Long-term for most lenders means five to seven years; short-term means one year or less; medium-term is anything in between.

Because you have to pay interest on debt, you should try to manage with as little as possible. However, few businesses get off the ground without putting some form of debt on their balance sheet. The issues are usually:

- What is the cheapest form of debt?
- What is the correct balance between debt and equity?
- How can you sensibly reduce the amount of borrowing required?
- To what extent must borrowing be backed by personal assets?

Matching Loans and Assets

It is a good idea to try to match the term of the loan to the type of asset that you are acquiring:

- To avoid constant renewing or restructuring problems

- To ensure that each loan is covered by the break-up value of the assets in case of disaster.

For example, a loan to buy premises should be a long-term loan, unless you can see clearly that you will have enough money within a short period to repay the loan. Taking out a short-term loan or overdraft to buy premises is a recipe for disaster. You may have to renegotiate it time and again – and, if your business runs into temporary difficulties, you run the risk of losing everything.

Short-term loans, or even overdrafts, are more suited to funding stock or debtors because you should be able to repay the loan once you have sold the goods or got the money in.

Short-term finance is also used to fund other forms of working capital and cash flow. It should always be repaid within the year – even if, at the end of the period, you still need to borrow more to fund future cash flow. In other words, your overdraft or short-term loan should be periodically cleared (or substantially reduced) by money coming in before you need to increase it again. If you have to borrow the same sum of money against the same asset for longer than a year at a time, you should be considering longer-term finance.

If disaster strikes and you have to repay the loan, it will be much easier to do so if the value of the assets is roughly equivalent to the outstanding value of the loan. Thus, for instance, you will hope to sell your premises for at least as much as you borrowed to buy them. Machinery may be more difficult, as the resale price is rarely comparable with the purchase price. For this reason (as well as because it's cheaper!), you should consider purchasing second-hand equipment for your start-up.

If you can, you should arrange your loans so that un-realisable assets are purchased out of your own equity, using borrowing only for realisable assets. If an asset is easily realisable, the bank is much more likely to accept it as security.

Other Sources

The main sources of loan finance (overdrafts, term loans and commercial mortgages) for start-ups are the banks. But don't look only to banks for debt. Credit unions may consider a small loan to get your business off the ground, particularly if you have been a regular saver.

As well as dealing with banks, you may also find yourself dealing with finance companies. Finance companies exist to lend money and make a return on it. They sometimes are more willing to lend than a bank, as long as they can secure the loan with assets or personal guarantees. They are not often cheaper than banks, but may sometimes be prepared to lend when banks refuse. This is not always a good thing. While it may shore up your own confidence in your project, it does not of itself increase the chances of success.

If you are having trouble getting finance, it may be an indication that you should reappraise your project. Talk to those who have refused you finance about their reasons before proceeding to other financiers. You may end up increasing your chances of success, both in raising finance the second time around and in the business itself.

Some finance companies (and foreign banks) specialise in certain types of finance, or special industry sectors. Because of their greater expertise and knowledge, they may be able to give you a better deal than the main retail banks because they understand your situation better.

When looking for finance, beware of 'specialists' who claim that they can find you money at favourable rates of interest if you pay an up-front fee. Don't ever pay any 'finder's fee' until you have received the money from the lending institution.

Expanding Your Credit Line

When (or, preferably, before) you have exhausted the borrowing facilities that your bank is prepared to provide (your credit line), you should consider two other forms of financing: leasing and factoring.

Leasing is particularly attractive as a way of acquiring the use of fixed assets – for example, plant and machinery, cars, office equipment – with the minimum up-front cost. Instead, you pay a regular monthly or quarterly payment, which is usually allowable for tax purposes. At the end of the lease, depending on the terms of the particular lease, you may have the option to continue using the asset for a modest continuing payment or to buy it outright from the leasing company.

Factoring, or invoice discounting, is a means of raising working capital, by 'selling' your debtors. The factoring company (usually a division or subsidiary of a bank – check with their small business unit) will pay you, say, 80 per cent of the face value of an invoice when it is issued. The balance, less charges, will be paid to you when the debt is settled. This form of financing is especially useful for the company that is rapidly expanding and in danger of being choked for lack of cash flow.

Who to Approach?

Who you approach for funds will depend on:

- How much finance you need
- What you need finance for
- Your company's risk profile.

Often, if you only need a small amount of money, the best way to raise it is still to approach a lender with which you have already built up some relationship, whether on a personal basis or in a business capacity. The larger borrower may feel it worthwhile to seek professional help to put together a more sophisticated finance package. Your accountant is the best person to give you advice in this area and may have contacts that will ease your path.

DEALING WITH BANKS

Whatever the means of finance you adopt, you will almost certainly have to deal with a bank for your daily needs, if not for your whole financial package.

Banks are conservative institutions with fixed procedures. You will hopefully have laid a good foundation for your business relationship with the bank by the way in which you have handled your personal finances. In smaller towns, you may already be well-known to the bank manager.

However, the relationship that your business will have with the bank is likely to be different from any personal relationship that you had with them before. You probably had a regular, guaranteed income going into your personal account. You may have had an overdraft, a mortgage, or perhaps a personal loan, but unless you were careless with your finances, the risk of getting into serious financial difficulty was slight.

In dealing with you as a business, some of the personal element disappears from the relationship and is replaced by an 'unknown risk' factor.

This risk factor stems from the following facts:

- The business is (usually) a separate legal entity from yourself and has no previous relationship with the bank

- The business has no guaranteed income (to the extent that your previous employment was secure, your personal income was 'guaranteed' – it no longer is, and don't be surprised if that changes your bank manager's attitude towards your own personal account)

- A high proportion of new businesses fail or experience financial difficulty for a variety of reasons that are difficult to predict

- The amount you have borrowed from the bank – for which the bank manager is ultimately responsible to the bank's shareholders – is likely to be much larger than any personal loan you have had in the past.

The more of the unknown risk that you are able to eliminate for the bank manager, the more the bank manager will be able to do for you, both in terms of providing the money you want and, in many cases, by giving you the benefit of their experience in commenting on your plans (see **Chapter 3**, *How a Financier Reads a Business Plan*).

The sort of information you can supply includes:

- A business plan, and updates when necessary
- Regular reports on the financial state of your business
- Information on a timely basis about any emerging problems that are going to result in late repayments, choked cash flow or a need for additional funding. A problem many bankers mention is that clients do not tell the bank what is wrong until the situation has grown so terrible that it is too late to correct
- Encouraging your banker to visit on-site to see for him/herself.

It is also true that too many bankers put a lot of effort into the initial analysis of a start-up loan, but fail to keep a close enough eye on their investment thereafter.

You can gain the maximum amount of assistance from your bank, not only by keeping the manager informed, but also by asking occasionally for an opinion of the financial outcome of a certain course of action. You should certainly have a face-to-face chat with your banker at least twice a year, and once a quarter if you can arrange it.

Other Points

If your business plan is approved and you are awarded your loan, overdraft, etc.:

- Don't be afraid to negotiate for the best possible terms. Most entrepreneurs will haggle happily over the price of a computer but will accept a bank's terms like lambs

- It may be a good idea to have an accountant or solicitor look at any loan agreement before you sign it. They may spot gaps, or unnecessary clauses, and their professional backing will give you added confidence in arguing your case

- Make all payments on time and in the agreed manner. If, for some reason, you will be late with a repayment, at least warn the bank in advance and, if possible, discuss the reasons with your bank manager.

Security

Providing security – pledging assets against a loan in case you are unable to repay it – is an ongoing issue (and a most vexatious one) between the small business community and the banks. Small business owners often feel it unjust that a large corporation can borrow a huge amount of money often without providing security, while they have to produce security for small loans.

Ideally, bankers will look for security in the business itself – premises, equipment or stock – but often small businesses rent their premises, lease their equipment and hold limited quantities of stock. Business machinery is not always suitable as security because it may have a low resale value, or may be built into the building where it is housed, making it difficult for the bank to sell it, if necessary, without incurring substantial additional costs. For this reason, a bank will sometimes seek personal guarantees, that is, the pledge of personal assets against business loans.

Beware of personal guarantees. A personal guarantee is exactly that. You are guaranteeing that, if the company cannot pay back the loan to the bank, you will do so. *How?* Think about it carefully before you sign.

Try to avoid giving a personal guarantee. It is probably better to borrow less, or pay a higher rate of interest, or use leasing as a means of financing specific fixed assets, than to be saddled with a personal guarantee.

As a condition of a loan, you may be asked by the bank not to pay any dividends or repay any other loans (especially ones you have made personally to the company) until the bank has been repaid. Though this is less onerous than a personal guarantee, only agree if these conditions are reasonable.

Check that whatever legal document you sign agrees with what you agreed with your bank manager. And, if the condition is for a limited period of time or until the loan is repaid, don't be shy about asking to be released from it when you have done your part and repaid the bank.

OTHER FINANCE

Although equity and debt represent the classic academic forms of financing, entrepreneurs are less concerned about such distinctions and are perfectly happy to consider sources of finance not listed in textbooks, for example:

- Enterprise competition prizes

- Grants from the Government, EU or private sector organisations listed in **Chapters 5** (England), **6** (Scotland), **7** (Wales), **8** (Northern Ireland), and **9** (EU support).

5

SUPPORT FOR START-UPS IN ENGLAND

In doing the research for this book, I was struck forcibly by the vast numbers of organisations operating in the 'enterprise/small business space', all dedicated to helping would-be entrepreneurs to get started and existing entrepreneurs to develop their businesses.

I was already aware broadly of the scope of enterprise support in Britain, from working with Terry Owens of *InBiz* to adapt our **Starting Your Own Business** workbook to UK needs. But it was only when I began to put the information down on paper that I realised what a maze the average entrepreneur faces!

The simplest way through this maze is to identify the organisations that support entrepreneurs by the type of support they provide (clearly, some organisations fit into more than one category).

The categories I have used are:

- Accountants
- Business Angels
- Business Plans
- Community & Rural Development
- Competitions
- Consultants
- Co-operatives
- Debt
- E-Business
- Enterprise Support
- Equity
- Franchises
- Grants
- Incubator
- Information
- Intellectual Property
- Inwards Investment
- Legal
- Marketing
- Mentoring
- Minorities & Disabilities
- Networking
- Policy
- Publications
- R&D
- Regulator & Standards
- Social Economy
- Start-Up Training
- Training

- Website
- Women
- Young Enterprise

What each of these categories covers is explained in this chapter. This means that, even if you live somewhere in the UK other than in England, you should still read this chapter to understand the categories.

The **Directory of Sources of Assistance** provides contact details and a brief description of the activities of each of the organisations included.

Note that the **Directory** is not – could not possibly be! – comprehensive. There are just too many organisations and sources of assistance to compile them all in one place – and the listing would quickly go out of date! Instead, this book sets you on the right path to a range of useful sources – for more information and updates, check the companion website, **www.startingabusinessinbritain.com**, from time to time.

ACCOUNTANTS

Accountants provide a variety of services to start-ups. They can assist and advise you on:

- The legal structure, taxation and accounting systems suitable for your business

- Business planning (though you should not let your accountant write your business plan – after all, it's your plan, not theirs!)

- Fund-raising and/or funding applications to banks, venture capitalists and grant-giving organisations.

In addition, where your turnover requires it, you must have an accountant to audit your business's annual accounts (see **Chapter 10).**

The four largest accounting firms in the UK (source: *Accountancy* magazine, June 2002), each of which has a small business unit, are:

* Deloitte & Touche
* Ernst & Young
* KPMG
* PriceWaterhouseCoopers.

There are then hundreds of other firms of accountants all across the UK. See **Chapter 10** on *Choosing an Accountant*, or contact one of the professional accounting bodies for the names of their members in your area:

* Association of Chartered Certified Accountants
* Chartered Institute of Management Accountants
* Institute of Chartered Accountants in England & Wales.

BUSINESS ANGELS

As noted in **Chapter 4**, Business Angels take their name from the world of theatre, where private investors who provide financing for shows in the early stages when success is less than certain are known as 'angels'. Business angels are usually experienced business-people, willing to invest both money and time in a start-up with potential. Note that they are rarely passive investors.

Business angels are hard to find. The **Directory** lists a number of organisations that have developed registers of such investors, though it is unlikely that they will allow you direct access to the investors without some screening process.

Business Angel organisations in England include:
- First Tuesday
- National Business Angels Network
- South Yorkshire Investment Fund.

BUSINESS PLANS

As **Chapter 3** makes clear, a business plan is essential for every start-up, regardless of its size, potential or the background of the promoters.

The **Directory** lists organisations that assist entrepreneurs, directly or indirectly, with developing a business plan. The caveats already expressed about doing it yourself apply.

The organisations include:
- Bplans.org.uk
- Harcourt Business Systems
- Ibis Associates
- Palo Alto Software.

COMMUNITY & RURAL DEVELOPMENT

A sizeable element of the support for enterprise in Britain comes from efforts towards community development, particularly where these are aimed at replacing industries that have closed down or relocated (or reducing dependence on them in advance).

The **Directory** lists organisations active in this area, as well as those active more generally in rural development.
- Advantage West Midlands (Regional Development Agency for the West Midlands)
- Bridges Community Ventures Ltd
- Community Action Network
- Department for Environment, Food & Rural Affairs

- Development Trusts Association
- East Midlands Development Agency
- East of England Development Agency
- London Development Agency
- North West Regional Development Agency
- OneNorthEast (Regional Development Agency for the North East)
- Rural Community Enterprise
- South East of England Development Agency
- South West Regional Development Agency
- UK LEADER +
- Yorkshire Forward (Regional Development Agency for Yorkshire & the Humber region).

COMPETITIONS

In addition to the youth/student-focused enterprise competitions identified in **Chapter 1**, which are aimed at introducing participants to the world of business, the **Directory** identifies a number of competitions and awards aimed at real-world entrepreneurs.

If you're eligible, it's often worth applying. Even if you don't win (and not everyone can, obviously), you often have to go through a useful screening/review process that can help you to identify ways in which you can improve aspects of your business. You also can make useful contacts among the other participants or the judges. And, if you do win, there's usually good publicity to be gained from an award, if you're ready to capitalise on it – and the prize money is always useful!

Competitions include:

- Growing Business Awards
- Imperial College Entrepreneurship Centre
- Oxford Science Enterprise Centre

- Shell LiveWIRE
- Women Mean Business Awards
- Young Enterprise.

CONSULTANTS

As a quick look at any telephone directory will show, there are hundreds, even thousands, of consultants – with a bewildering array of expertise – available to help you to develop your start-up business and make it grow.

Use consultants carefully. Know what you want them to do, when, and at what cost to you. Make sure they deliver before you sign off and pay their fees.

Look for the consultant who thinks long-term – and is prepared to invest in you and your future success. Look for a consultant with practical experience in your area of business – you do not want to pay for their learning!

But recognise that consultants must eat too – if you want work done, you must be prepared to pay for it. Free advice will not take you far!

To find a consultant, look to:

- Chartered Institute of Management Accountants
- Consultants Register
- Deloitte & Touche
- Ernst & Young
- Institute of Business Advisers
- KPMG
- Nuventis Partners
- PriceWaterhouseCoopers
- Project NorthEast.

Co-operatives

In choosing a structure for your new business, you may want to consider the co-operative model for a democratically controlled business.

Organisations that promote the co-operative concept and/or assist in their formation include:

• Industrial Common Ownership Movement Limited.

Debt

It's hard to get started without some borrowings. The following are some of the (many) sources of debt finance in England:

• Abbey National
• Alliance & Leicester Business Banking
• Allied Irish Bank (GB)
• Association of British Credit Unions Ltd
• Bank of Ireland UK
• Bank of Scotland Ltd
• Barclays Bank
• Bristol & West PLC
• Clydesdale Bank PLC
• Co-operative Bank PLC
• HSBC
• Lloyds TSB Bank PLC
• NatWest
• Prince's Trust
• Royal Bank of Scotland PLC
• Royal British Legion Small Business Advisory & Loan Scheme
• Small Firms Loan Guarantee Scheme
• South Yorkshire Investment Fund
• Spirit of Enterprise Fund

- Triodos Bank
- UK Steel Enterprise Ltd
- West Midlands Finance
- Yorkshire Bank PLC.

Again, to repeat the warning in **Chapter 4**, beware of anyone who promises to obtain finance for you for a fee – there are plenty of lenders all looking for your business, so you shouldn't have to pay anyone to find a lender for you.

E-BUSINESS

The bloom has definitely faded from the e-business 'gold rush' that marked the end of the last millennium. A sad, but harsh, truth was learnt by the early e-entrepreneurs (and their investors) – that you have to make a profit to stay in business and that profits require a business model that works (back to planning!).

Nonetheless, technology is changing the way we live and do business. The Directory lists initiatives and sources of advice or assistance in this area. Many of these are aimed at providing small businesses with the tools and techniques to succeed in this new age.

Support in England includes:

- First Tuesday.

ENTERPRISE SUPPORT

A 'catch-all' category for organisations that provide support that does not fit into any of the other categories or spans beyond them, it mainly applies to national/regional enterprise support organisations, such as:

- Advantage West Midlands
- East Midlands Development Agency

- East of England Development Agency
- Local Enterprise Agencies
- London Development Agency
- National Federation of Enterprise Agencies.
- North West Regional Development Agency
- OneNorthEast
- South East of England Development Agency
- South West Regional Development Agency
- Yorkshire Forward.

EQUITY

Equity, as **Chapter 4** made clear, is the life-blood of any business. If you haven't enough of your own, you must find some elsewhere. Some of the (many) sources of equity, or of finding those who provide equity, include:

- 3I Group PLC
- Apax Partners Ltd
- British Venture Capital Association
- Business Innovation Centres
- Capital Fund
- Creative Advantage Fund
- Mercia Enterprise Fund
- National Business Angels Network
- Phoenix Fund
- Project NorthEast
- Regional Venture Funds
- South Yorkshire Investment Fund
- UK Steel Enterprise Ltd
- West Midlands Finance.

FRANCHISES

Franchises have a major attraction over starting a business from scratch – their success rate can be as high as 90%, against the 50% for start-ups generally. This is because the underlying business model has already been tested in a variety of situations before you invest in the franchise.

Sources of information on franchises in England include:

* British Franchise Association
* FranchiseDirect.com
* MyFranchise.net
* WhichFranchise.com.

GRANTS

Grants should be handled with care. Usually, there are conditions to be met (rightly so, since it's taxpayers' money that's being used) but beware that meeting the conditions does not drive your business in a direction that you do not want to go.

That said, grants are a major boost to a start-up or early-stage businesses – not just because of the money but also because of the endorsement they imply.

Some of the many sources of grants (or sources of directions to grants) in England are:

* Advantage West Midlands
* East Midlands Development Agency
* East of England Development Agency
* Grantfinder
* j4b.co.uk
* London Development Agency
* North West Regional Development Agency
* OneNorthEast

- Prince's Trust
- Regional Selective Assistance
- SMART
- South East of England Development Agency
- South West Regional Development Agency
- West Midlands Finance
- Yorkshire Forward.

INCUBATOR

Chapter 1 makes the case for incubators, especially for high-tech start-ups. There are major initiatives underway across Britain to put incubators in place – inquire from the organisations below or at your local *Business Link*:

- Advantage West Midlands
- Business Innovation Centres
- East Midlands Development Agency
- East of England Development Agency
- London Development Agency
- North West Regional Development Agency
- OneNorthEast
- Project NorthEast
- South East of England Development Agency
- South West Regional Development Agency
- UK Business Incubation
- Universities (check locally)
- Yorkshire Forward.

INFORMATION

Information is critical to a well-planned and managed start-up. Potential sources of market research information were identified in **Chapter 2**. The **Directory** expands on these, giving you a headstart in finding out what you need to know.

Recognise that some of these organisations are member-based and restrict their services to members only, or charge fees to non-members. Most of the organisations listed are key players in their own industries, with a good finger on what's happening – it may be well worth your while paying for their specialist insight.

Some of the (many) sources of information relevant to start-ups in England are:

- African Caribbean Business Forum
- Asian Business Forum
- Aurora Women's Network
- Beermat Entrepreneur
- Better-business.co.uk
- Beyond Bricks Ecademy
- BizWise.co.uk
- British Association of Women Entrepreneurs
- British Chambers of Commerce
- Business Bureau UK
- Business Innovation Centres
- Business Link
- ClearlyBusiness.co.uk
- Companies House
- eGrindstone.co.uk
- Environment Agency
- European Information Centres
- Everywoman.co.uk

- EW-Network
- FastLinkSolutions.co.uk
- Forum of Private Business
- FranchiseDirect.com
- Getfinance.co.uk
- Grantfinder
- Health & Safety Executive
- HM Customs & Excise
- Home Business Alliance
- Inland Revenue
- Innovateur
- Institute for Small Business Affairs
- Institute of Directors
- j4b.co.uk
- Local Enterprise Agencies
- Mintel International Group Ltd
- MyFranchise.net
- New Business - New Life
- Patent Office
- Royal British Legion Small Business Advisory & Loan Scheme
- Rural Community Enterprise
- SeekingFinance.co.uk
- SFEDI - Small Firms Enterprise Development Initiative
- SmallBiz UK.com
- SmallBusiness.co.uk
- SmallBusinessAdvice.org.uk
- Startbusiness.co.uk
- StartInBusiness.co.uk
- StartingaBusinessinBritain.com
- Startups.co.uk

- Success4Business
- The-Bag-Lady.co.uk
- The-SME.co.uk
- Trade Partners UK
- Trading Standards Institute
- UK Business Incubation
- UK Online
- West Midlands Finance
- WhichFranchise.com.

INTELLECTUAL PROPERTY

Intellectual property is a catch-all phrase used to describe the various rights conferred by patents, trade marks, copyright, etc. Under UK and EU law, you can protect your 'rights' in inventions and so on (but not in ideas alone).

You can then exploit these rights yourself or license or sell them to others – this is called 'technology transfer'. Technology transfer also works on an inwards basis, with British businesses acquiring rights to use technologies developed elsewhere.

It's a specialist area in which you should take advice and proceed with caution.

Sources of information and advice in England include:

- Intellectual Property UK
- Patent Office.

INWARDS INVESTMENT

Inwards investment refers to the attraction of investment, in businesses creating jobs locally, usually in areas lacking in other employment opportunities. Organisations involved in inwards investment in England include:

- Advantage West Midlands
- East Midlands Development Agency
- East of England Development Agency
- London Development Agency
- North West Regional Development Agency
- OneNorthEast
- South East of England Development Agency
- South West Regional Development Agency
- Yorkshire Forward.

LEGAL

It's useful for a start-up to have access to good legal advice. To find a solicitor, contact:

- Law Society
- Lawyers for Your Business.

MARKETING

Despite significant improvements in this area (driven in part by the organisations listed below), survey after survey shows that a consistent failing of British business has been – and still is – its lack of emphasis on, and commitment to, marketing.

Organisations that can support small businesses' own marketing efforts include:

- Business Innovation Centres
- Mintel International Group Ltd.

Check also under 'Training' for providers of courses in marketing.

MENTORING

A key support offered by many support agencies now is mentoring – the provision of an experienced business-person with skills, be they specialist or general, appropriate to the needs of the mentored business/entrepreneur at the time.

Mentors are neither consultants nor executives. They do not carry the burden of responsibility involved in running a business, nor are they paid to do a specific task or job in it. Their role is to share their experience – all mentors are experienced business-people – to assist the entrepreneur in coming to their own decisions.

The **Directory** lists organisations in England that provide mentoring, often a part of a broader package of supports:

- British Association of Women Entrepreneurs
- Business Volunteer Mentoring Association
- Institute of Business Advisers
- National Federation of Enterprise Agencies
- South Yorkshire Investment Fund.

MINORITIES & DISABILITIES

Organisations in England committed to assisting minorities or those with disabilities to fulfil their potential as entrepreneurs include:

- African Caribbean Business Forum
- Asian Business Forum
- Black Training & Enterprise Group
- Institute of Asian Businesses
- Minority Business Form
- Spirit of Enterprise Fund.

NETWORKING

The Directory identifies a large number of organisations that provide networking opportunities or facilitate them – sometimes for members only, since many of these are the same key industry player organisations that were a source of market research and other information earlier.

If you're not out and about meeting people for some part of your time, you're probably missing opportunities to meet potential customers, to find out what competitors are up to, or to spot new business leads.

Networking opportunities in England include:

- Aurora Women's Network
- British Association of Women Entrepreneurs
- British Chambers of Commerce
- Confederation of British Business
- Entrepreneurs' Network Club
- everywoman.co.uk
- EW-Network
- Federation of Small Businesses
- First Tuesday
- Forum of Private Business
- Home Business Alliance
- Institute for Small Business Affairs
- Institute of Directors
- PLATO England
- UK Business Incubation.

POLICY

Although far from the minds of most entrepreneurs, policy is critical to creating an environment in which enterprise can flourish. The organisations below are responsible for setting and monitoring the implementation of policy in England:

- Advantage West Midlands
- African Caribbean Business Forum
- Asian Business Forum
- Black Training & Enterprise Group
- Department for Environment, Food & Rural Affairs
- Department for Work & Pensions
- Department of Trade & Industry
- East Midlands Development Agency
- East of England Development Agency
- Government Offices
- Institute for Small Business Affairs
- London Development Agency
- North West Regional Development Agency
- OneNorthEast
- Small Business Service
- South East of England Development Agency
- South West Regional Development Agency
- Yorkshire Forward.

PUBLICATIONS

As a writer and publisher, publications of all kinds are always of interest to me personally. But they should be of interest to you too – as a source of information, a replacement for training (some, not all), and as a means of developing yourself.

Useful publications (or sources of them) include:

- Beermat Entrepreneur
- Better-business.co.uk
- Oak Tree Press.

R&D

Research & Development – and support for it – is critical to the development of technology businesses. There's an increasing level of support, as the **Directory** shows:

- Chartered Institute of Patent Agents
- Isis Innovation Ltd
- London innovation
- National Endowment for Science, technology & the Arts
- SMART
- The virtual company
- UK Science Parks Association.

REGULATOR & STANDARDS

Increasingly, both regulators and standards-setters are approachable and informative – for example, the Inland Revenue produces an award-winning start-up guide and, in many other ways, provide early assistance and encouragement towards developing the habit of compliance rather than merely enforcing it by rule of law subsequently.

The **Directory** identifies key regulatory and standards-setting bodies in England of interest and relevance to start-ups and small businesses, including:

- Companies House
- Environment Agency
- Health & Safety Executive

- HM Customs & Excise
- Inland Revenue
- Investors in People
- Patent Office
- SFEDI - Small Firms Enterprise Development Initiative
- Trading Standards Institute.

SOCIAL ECONOMY

The social economy is that part of the economy lying between the public and private sector – it includes many of the not-for-profit organisations and voluntary groups that do so much good. The organisations below assist entrepreneurs develop social enterprises:

- Community Action Network
- Industrial Common Ownership Movement Limited
- London Development Agency
- Rural Community Enterprise
- School for Social Entrepreneurs
- Seo-Online.org.uk
- Social Enterprise London.

START-UP TRAINING

Sources of start-up training in England include:

- DHP Enterprise
- InBiz
- Jobcentre Plus
- National Extension College
- Oak Tree Press
- Prince's Trust.

In addition, *Universities* and other educational institutions provide courses – inquire locally.

TRAINING

It's not enough to start a business – in some ways, difficult as it may be, that's the easy bit! – you also have to keep it going. And as you do, you will discover that you need new skills or to develop existing skills further – you need training on an on-going basis.

Most professional bodies have long since identified this requirement and have made a point of continuing training being a condition of membership. You could do worse than adopt the same high standards for your new profession of entrepreneur. And the **Directory** will help with some useful sources, depending on your own specific needs and circumstances:

- British Chambers of Commerce
- Business Innovation Centres
- Durham Business School
- Ibis Associates
- InBiz
- Industrial Common Ownership Movement Limited
- Institute of Business Advisers
- Institute of Directors
- Institute of Leadership & Management
- Learn Direct for Business
- Learning & Skills Council
- National Extension College
- Oak Tree Press
- PLATO England
- Project NorthEast

- School for Social Entrepreneurs
- SEED
- Trading Standards Institute.

WEBSITE

The Internet is now a major source of information for entrepreneurs. The UK Government is committed to communicating online with its citizens – see *UK Online.co.uk*. Other sources for entrepreneurs in England include:

- Aurora Women's Network
- Better-business.co.uk
- Beyond Bricks Ecademy
- BizWise.co.uk
- Bplans.org.uk
- Business Bureau UK
- Business Link
- ClearlyBusiness.co.uk
- eGrindstone.co.uk
- Everywoman.co.uk
- EW-Network
- FastLinkSolutions.co.uk
- Getfinance.co.uk
- Grantfinder
- HM Customs & Excise
- Inland Revenue
- Innovateur
- j4b.co.uk
- New Business - New Life
- Oak Tree Press
- SeekingFinance.co.uk

- SmallBiz UK.com
- SmallBusiness.co.uk
- SmallBusinessAdvice.org.uk
- Startbusiness.co.uk
- StartInBusiness.co.uk
- StartingaBusinessinBritain.com
- Startups.co.uk
- Success4Business
- The-Bag-Lady.co.uk
- The-SME.co.uk
- UK Online
- West Midlands Finance
- WhichFranchise.com.

WOMEN

My research identified a number of organisations that specifically catered for the needs of women entrepreneurs:

- Aurora Women's Network
- British Association of Women Entrepreneurs
- Everywoman.co.uk
- EW-Network
- SEED
- The-Bag-Lady.co.uk
- Women Mean Business Awards.

YOUNG ENTERPRISE

Encouraging young people to start businesses, or even planting the seed of the idea at an early stage, is an important part of developing an 'enterprise culture'. Organisations engaged in this work in England include:

- Prince's Trust
- Project NorthEast
- Shell LiveWIRE
- Young Enterprise.

6

SUPPORT FOR START-UPS IN SCOTLAND

This chapter is organised in the same category structure as **Chapter 5**, in which each of these categories is explained. This means that, even if you live somewhere in the UK other than in England, you should still read **Chapter 5** to understand the categories.

This chapter identifies both national sources of support and those specific to Scotland alone in each category.

The **Directory of Sources of Assistance** provides contact details and a brief description of the activities of each of the organisations included.

ACCOUNTANTS

Accounting firms:

- Deloitte & Touche
- Ernst & Young
- KPMG
- PriceWaterhouseCoopers.

Professional accounting bodies:

- Association of Chartered Certified Accountants
- Chartered Institute of Management Accountants
- Institute of Chartered Accountants in Scotland.

BUSINESS ANGELS

- Equitygap Ltd
- First Tuesday Scotland
- LINC Scotland
- National Business Angels Network
- Young Company Finance.

BUSINESS PLANS

- Bplans.org.uk
- Harcourt Business Systems
- Ibis Associates
- Palo Alto Software.

COMMUNITY & RURAL DEVELOPMENT

- Community Action Network
- Department for Environment, Food & Rural Affairs
- Development Trusts Association
- Rural Community Enterprise
- UK LEADER +.

COMPETITIONS

- Growing Business Awards
- Shell LiveWIRE
- Women Mean Business Awards
- Young Enterprise Scotland.

CONSULTANTS

- Chartered Institute of Management Accountants
- Consultants Register
- Deloitte & Touche
- Ernst & Young
- Institute of Business Advisers
- KPMG
- PriceWaterhouseCoopers
- Project NorthEast.

CO-OPERATIVES

- Industrial Common Ownership Movement Limited.

DEBT

- Abbey National
- Alliance & Leicester Business Banking
- Allied Irish Bank (GB)
- Association of British Credit Unions Ltd
- Bank of Ireland UK
- Bank of Scotland Ltd
- Barclays Bank

- Bristol & West PLC
- Co-operative Bank PLC
- HSBC
- Lloyds TSB Bank PLC
- Prince's Scottish Youth Business Trust
- Royal Bank of Scotland PLC
- Royal British Legion Small Business Advisory & Loan Scheme
- Small Firms Loan Guarantee Scheme
- Triodos Bank.

E-BUSINESS

- First Tuesday Scotland.

ENTERPRISE SUPPORT

- Highlands & Islands Enterprise
- Scottish Development International
- Scottish Enterprise
- Scottish Enterprise Network.

EQUITY

- 3I Group PLC
- Apax Partners Ltd
- British Venture Capital Association
- Business Innovation Centres
- Equitygap Ltd
- LINC Scotland Ltd
- Phoenix Fund
- Scottish Equity Partners Ltd.

FRANCHISES

- British Franchise Association
- FranchiseDirect.com
- MyFranchise.net
- WhichFranchise.com.

GRANTS

- Grantfinder
- j4b.co.uk
- Prince's Scottish Youth Business Trust
- Regional Selective Assistance Scotland
- SMART:Scotland.

INCUBATOR

- Business Innovation Centres
- UK Business Incubation.

INFORMATION

- Aurora Women's Network
- Beermat Entrepreneur
- Better-business.co.uk
- Beyond Bricks Ecademy
- BioTech-Scotland
- BizWise.co.uk
- British Association of Women Entrepreneurs
- British Chambers of Commerce
- Business Bureau UK

- Business Information Source in Highland Scotland
- Business Innovation Centres
- ClearlyBusiness.co.uk
- Companies House
- eGrindstone.co.uk
- European Information Centres
- Everywoman.co.uk
- EW-Network
- FastLinkSolutions.co.uk
- Forum of Private Business in Scotland
- FranchiseDirect.com
- Getfinance.co.uk
- Grantfinder
- Health & Safety Executive
- Highlands and Islands Enterprise
- HM Customs & Excise
- Home Business Alliance
- Inland Revenue
- Innovateur
- Institute for Small Business Affairs
- Institute of Directors
- j4b.co.uk
- Mintel International Group Ltd,
- MyFranchise.net
- National Federation of Enterprise Agencies
- New Business - New Life
- Patent Office
- Royal British Legion Small Business Advisory & Loan Scheme
- Rural Community Enterprise
- Scottish Chambers of Commerce

- Scottish Enterprise
- Scottish Enterprise Network
- Scottish Environment Protection Agency
- ScottishBusinessWomen.com
- SFEDI - Small Firms Enterprise Development Initiative
- Small Business Gateway for Lowlands Scotland
- SmallBiz UK.com
- SmallBusiness.co.uk
- SmallBusinessAdvice.org.uk
- Startbusiness.co.uk
- StartInBusiness.co.uk
- StartingaBusinessinBritain.com
- Startups.co.uk
- Success4Business
- The-Bag-Lady.co.uk
- The-SME.co.uk
- Trade Partners UK
- Trading Standards Institute
- UK Business Incubation
- UK Online
- WhichFranchise.com
- Young Company Finance.

INTELLECTUAL PROPERTY

- Intellectual Property UK
- Patent Office.

INWARDS INVESTMENT

- Scottish Development International.

LEGAL

- Law Society of Scotland
- Lawyers for Your Business.

MARKETING

- Business Innovation Centres
- Mintel International Group Ltd.

MENTORING

- British Association of Women Entrepreneurs
- Business Mentoring Scotland
- Business Volunteer Mentoring Association
- Institute of Business Advisers
- National Federation of Enterprise Agencies
- Targeting Technology Limited.

NETWORKING

- British Association of Women Entrepreneurs
- British Chambers of Commerce
- Confederation of British Business
- Entrepreneurial Exchange
- everywoman.co.uk
- EW-Network

- Federation of Small Businesses
- First Tuesday Scotland
- Forum of Private Business in Scotland
- Home Business Alliance
- Institute for Small Business Affairs
- Institute of Directors
- Scottish Chambers of Commerce
- UK Business Innovation.

POLICY

- Department for Environment, Food & Rural Affairs
- Department for Work & Pensions
- Department of Trade & Industry
- Institute for Small Business Affairs
- Scottish Executive
- Small Business Service.

PUBLICATIONS

- Beermat Entrepreneur
- Better-business.co.uk
- Oak Tree Press
- Young Company Finance.

R&D

- BioTech-Scotland
- Chartered Institute of Patent Agents
- ICASS
- National Endowment for Science, Technology & the Arts

- Scottish Institute for Enterprise
- SMART:Scotland
- Targeting Technology ltd
- Technology Ventures Scotland
- UK Science Parks Association.

REGULATOR & STANDARDS

- Companies House
- Health & Safety Executive
- HM Customs & Excise
- Inland Revenue
- Investors in People
- Patent Office
- Scottish Environment Protection Agency
- SFEDI - Small Firms Enterprise Development Initiative
- Trading Standards Institute.

SOCIAL ECONOMY

- Community Action Network
- Industrial Common Ownership Movement Limited
- Rural Community Enterprise
- School for Social Entrepreneurs
- Seo-Online.org.uk.

START-UP TRAINING

- DHP Enterprise
- Get Into Enterprise
- Jobcentre Plus

- National Extension College
- Oak Tree Press
- Prince's Scottish Youth Business Trust.

TRAINING

- British Chambers of Commerce
- Business Innovation Centres
- Durham Business School
- Ibis Associates
- Industrial Common Ownership Movement Limited
- Institute of Business Advisers
- Institute of Directors
- Institute of Leadership & Management
- Learn Direct for Business
- Learning & Skills Council
- National Extension College
- Oak Tree Press
- School for Social Entrepreneurs
- Scottish Chambers of Commerce
- SEED
- Trading Standards Institute
- Wellpark Enterprise Centre
- Your People Manager.

WEBSITE

- Aurora Women's Network
- Better-business.co.uk
- Beyond Bricks Ecademy

- BizWise.co.uk
- Bplans.org.uk
- Business Bureau UK
- Business Information Source in Highland Scotland
- ClearlyBusiness.co.uk
- eGrindstone.co.uk
- Everywoman.co.uk
- EW-Network
- FastLinkSolutions.co.uk
- Getfinance.co.uk
- Grantfinder
- Highlands & Islands Enterprise
- HM Customs & Excise
- Inland Revenue
- Innovateur
- j4b.co.uk
- New Business - New Life
- Oak Tree Press
- Scottish Enterprise
- ScottishBusinessWomen.com
- Small Business Gateway for Lowland Scotland
- SmallBiz UK.com
- SmallBusiness.co.uk
- SmallBusinessAdvice.org.uk
- Startbusiness.co.uk
- StartInBusiness.co.uk
- StartingaBusinessinBritain.com
- Startups.co.uk
- Success4Business
- The-Bag-Lady.co.uk

- The-SME.co.uk
- UK Online
- WhichFranchise.com.

WOMEN

- Aurora Women's Network
- British Association of Women Entrepreneurs
- Everywoman.co.uk
- EW-Network
- ScottishBusinessWomen.com
- SEED
- The-Bag-Lady.co.uk
- Wellpark Enterprise Centre
- Women Mean Business Awards.

YOUNG ENTERPRISE

- Prince's Scottish Youth Business Trust
- Shell LiveWIRE
- Young Enterprise Scotland.

7

SUPPORT FOR START-UPS IN WALES

This chapter is organised in the same category structure as **Chapter 5**, in which each of these categories is explained. This means that, even if you live somewhere in the UK other than in England, you should still read **Chapter 5** to understand the categories.

This chapter identifies both national sources of support and those specific to Wales alone in each category.

The **Directory of Sources of Assistance** provides contact details and a brief description of the activities of each of the organisations included.

ACCOUNTANTS

Accounting firms:

- Deloitte & Touche
- Ernst & Young
- KPMG
- PriceWaterhouseCoopers.

Professional accounting bodies:

- Association of Chartered Certified Accountants
- Chartered Institute of Management Accountants
- Institute of Chartered Accountants in England & Wales.

BUSINESS ANGELS

- First Tuesday
- National Business Angels Network.

BUSINESS PLANS

- Bplans.org.uk
- Harcourt Business Systems
- Ibis Associates
- Palo Alto Software.

COMMUNITY & RURAL DEVELOPMENT

- Community Action Network
- Department for Environment, Food & Rural Affairs
- Development Trusts Association
- Rural Community Enterprise
- UK LEADER +.

COMPETITIONS

- Growing Business Awards
- Shell LiveWIRE
- Women Mean Business Awards
- Young Enterprise.

CONSULTANTS

- Chartered Institute of Management Accountants
- Consultants Register
- Deloitte & Touche
- Ernst & Young
- Institute of Business Advisers
- KPMG
- PriceWaterhouseCoopers.

CO-OPERATIVES

- Industrial Common Ownership Movement Limited.

DEBT

- Abbey National
- Alliance & Leicester Business Banking
- Allied Irish Bank (GB)
- Association of British Credit Unions Ltd
- Bank of Ireland UK
- Bank of Scotland Ltd
- Barclays Bank
- Bristol & West PLC
- Co-operative Bank PLC
- HSBC
- Lloyds TSB Bank PLC
- NatWest
- Prince's Trust Cymru
- Royal Bank of Scotland PLC
- Royal British Legion Small Business Advisory & Loan Scheme

- Small Firms Loan Guarantee Scheme
- Triodos Bank.

E-BUSINESS

- First Tuesday
- Opportunity Wales.co.uk.

ENTERPRISE SUPPORT

- Local Enterprise Agencies
- National Federation of Enterprise Agencies
- Welsh Development Agency.

EQUITY

- 3i Group PLC
- Apax Partners Ltd
- British Venture Capital Association
- Business Innovation Centres
- Phoenix Fund.

FRANCHISES

- British Franchise Association
- FranchiseDirect.com
- MyFranchise.net
- WhichFranchise.com.

GRANTS

- Grantfinder
- j4b.co.uk
- Prince's Trust Cymru
- Regional Selective Assistance Wales
- SMART Wales.

INCUBATOR

- Business Innovation Centres
- UK Business Incubation.

INFORMATION

- Aurora Women's Network
- BecauseYouCan.com
- Beermat Entrepreneur
- Better-business.co.uk
- Beyond Bricks Ecademy
- BizWise.co.uk
- British Association of Women Entrepreneurs
- British Chambers of Commerce
- Business Bureau UK
- Business Connect Wales
- Business Innovation Centres
- ClearlyBusiness.co.uk
- Companies House
- eGrindstone.co.uk
- Environment Agency
- European Information Centres

- Everywoman.co.uk
- EW-Network
- FastLinkSolutions.co.uk
- Finance Wales
- Forum of Private Business
- FranchiseDirect.com
- Getfinance.co.uk
- Grantfinder
- Health & Safety Executive
- HM Customs & Excise
- Home Business Alliance
- Inland Revenue
- Innovateur
- Institute for Small Business Affairs
- Institute of Directors
- j4b.co.uk
- Local Enterprise Agencies
- Mintel International Group Ltd
- MyFranchise.net
- New Business - New Life
- Opportunity Wales.co.uk
- Patent Office
- Royal British Legion Small Business Advisory & Loan Scheme
- Rural Community Enterprise
- SFEDI - Small Firms Enterprise Development Initiative
- SmallBiz UK.com
- SmallBusiness.co.uk
- SmallBusinessAdvice.org.uk
- Startbusiness.co.uk
- StartInBusiness.co.uk

- StartingaBusinessinBritain.com
- Startups.co.uk
- Success4Business
- The-Bag-Lady.co.uk
- The-SME.co.uk
- Trade Partners UK
- Trading Standards Institute
- UK Business Incubation
- UK Online
- Welsh Development Agency
- WhichFranchise.com.

INTELLECTUAL PROPERTY

- Intellectual Property UK
- Patent Office.

INWARDS INVESTMENT

- Welsh Development Agency.

LEGAL

- Law Society
- Lawyers for Your Business.

MARKETING

- Business Innovation Centres
- Mintel International Group Ltd.

MENTORING

- British Association of Women Entrepreneurs
- Business Volunteer Mentoring Association
- Institute of Business Advisers
- Mentor Wales
- National Federation of Enterprise Agencies.

MINORITIES & DISABILITIES

- Potentia Cymru.

NETWORKING

- British Association of Women Entrepreneurs
- British Chambers of Commerce
- Confederation of British Business
- everywoman.co.uk
- EW-Network
- Federation of Small Businesses
- First Tuesday
- Forum of Private Business
- Home Business Alliance
- Institute for Small Business Affairs
- Institute of Directors
- UK Business Innovation.

POLICY

- Department for Environment, Food & Rural Affairs
- Department for Work & Pensions

- Department of Trade & Industry
- Institute for Small Business Affairs
- National Assembly of Wales
- Small Business Service.

PUBLICATIONS

- Beermat Entrepreneur
- Better-business.co.uk
- Oak Tree Press.

R&D

- Chartered Institute of Patent Agents
- National Endowment for Science, Technology & the Arts
- SMART Wales
- UK Science Park Association
- Wales Spinout Programme.

REGULATOR & STANDARDS

- Companies House
- Environment Agency
- Health & Safety Executive
- HM Customs & Excise
- Inland Revenue
- Investors in People
- Patent Office
- SFEDI - Small Firms Enterprise Development Initiative
- Trading Standards Institute.

SOCIAL ECONOMY

- Community Action Network
- Industrial Common Ownership Movement Limited
- School for Social Entrepreneurs
- Seo-Online.org.uk.

START-UP TRAINING

- Jobcentre Plus
- National Extension College
- Oak Tree Press
- Prince's Trust Cymru.

TRAINING

- British Chambers of Commerce
- Business Innovation Centres
- Durham Business School
- Ibis Associates
- Industrial Common Ownership Movement Limited
- Institute of Business Advisers
- Institute of Directors
- Institute of Leadership & Management
- Learn Direct for Business
- Learning & Skills Council
- National Extension College
- Oak Tree Press
- School for Social Entrepreneurs
- SEED
- Trading Standards Institute.

WEBSITE

- Aurora Women's Network
- BecauseYouCan.com
- Better-business.co.uk
- Beyond Bricks Ecademy
- BizWise.co.uk
- Bplans.org.uk
- Business Bureau UK
- Business Connect Wales
- ClearlyBusiness.co.uk
- eGrindstone.co.uk
- Everywoman.co.uk
- EW-Network
- FastLinkSolutions.co.uk
- Getfinance.co.uk
- Grantfinder
- HM Customs & Excise
- Inland Revenue
- Innovateur
- j4b.co.uk
- New Business - New Life
- Oak Tree Press
- SmallBiz UK.com
- SmallBusiness.co.uk
- SmallBusinessAdvice.org.uk
- Startbusiness.co.uk
- StartInBusiness.co.uk
- StartingaBusinessinBritain.com
- Startups.co.uk

- Success4Business
- The-Bag-Lady.co.uk
- The-SME.co.uk
- UK Online
- Welsh Development Agency
- WhichFranchise.com.

WOMEN

- Aurora Women's Network
- British Association of Women Entrepreneurs
- Everywoman.co.uk
- EW-Network
- SEED
- The-Bag-Lady.co.uk
- Women Mean Business Awards.

YOUNG ENTERPRISE

- Prince's Trust Cymru
- Shell LiveWIRE
- Young Enterprise.

8

SUPPORT FOR START-UPS IN NORTHERN IRELAND

This chapter is organised in the same category structure as **Chapter 5**, in which each of these categories is explained. This means that, even if you live somewhere in the UK other than in England, you should still read **Chapter 5** to understand the categories.

This chapter identifies both national sources of support and those specific to Northern Ireland alone in each category.

The **Directory of Sources of Assistance** provides contact details and a brief description of the activities of each of the organisations included.

ACCOUNTANTS

Accounting firms:

- Deloitte & Touche
- Ernst & Young
- KPMG
- PriceWaterhouseCoopers.

Professional accounting bodies:

- Association of Chartered Certified Accountants
- Chartered Institute of Management Accountants
- Institute of Chartered Accountants in Ireland.

BUSINESS ANGELS

- Equity Network
- First Tuesday.

BUSINESS PLANS

- Bplans.org.uk
- Harcourt Business Systems
- Ibis Associates
- Palo Alto Software.

COMMUNITY & RURAL DEVELOPMENT

- Department of Agriculture & Rural Development (NORTHERN IRELAND)
- Social Economy Agency
- UK LEADER +.

COMPETITIONS

- Growing Business Awards
- Shell LiveWIRE
- Young Enterprise Northern Ireland.

CONSULTANTS

- Chartered Institute of Management Accountants
- Consultants Register
- Deloitte & Touche
- Ernst & Young
- Institute of Business Advisers
- KPMG
- PriceWaterhouseCoopers.

DEBT

- Bank of Ireland Northern Ireland
- Bank of Scotland Ltd
- Barclays Bank
- Co-operative Bank PLC
- First Trust Bank
- HSBC
- Northern Bank Ltd
- Prince's Trust Northern Ireland
- Royal Bank of Scotland PLC
- Royal British Legion Small Business Advisory & Loan Scheme
- Small Firms Loan Guarantee Scheme
- Social Economy Agency
- Triodos Bank
- Ulster Bank.

E-BUSINESS

- First Tuesday
- TradeNetIreland.

ENTERPRISE SUPPORT

- InterTradeIreland
- InvestNI.

EQUITY

- 3i Group PLC
- Apax Partners Ltd
- British Venture Capital Association
- Business Innovation Centres
- Crescent Capital
- Equity Network
- Qubis Ltd.

FRANCHISES

- British Franchise Association
- FranchiseDirect.com
- MyFranchise.net
- WhichFranchise.com.

GRANTS

- Business Innovation Link
- Grantfinder

- j4b.co.uk
- Prince's Trust Northern Ireland
- Social Economy Agency
- UUTech Ltd.

INCUBATOR

- Business Innovation Centres
- UK Business Incubation
- UUTech Ltd.

INFORMATION

- Aurora Women's Network
- Beermat Entrepreneur
- Belfast First Stop Business Shop
- Better-business.co.uk
- Beyond Bricks Ecademy
- BizWise.co.uk
- British Association of Women Entrepreneurs
- Business Bureau UK
- Business Innovation Centres
- BusinessInformationPoint.com
- ClearlyBusiness.co.uk
- Companies Registry (NORTHERN IRELAND)
- eGrindstone.co.uk
- Enterprise Northern Ireland
- European Information Centres
- Everywoman.co.uk
- EW-Network

- FastLinkSolutions.co.uk
- FranchiseDirect.com
- Getfinance.co.uk
- Government Direct for Business
- Grantfinder
- Health & Safety Executive for Northern Ireland
- HM Customs & Excise
- Home Business Alliance
- Inland Revenue
- Innovateur
- Institute for Small Business Affairs
- Institute of Directors
- InterTradeIreland
- InvestNI
- j4b.co.uk
- Mintel International Group Ltd
- MyFranchise.net
- New Business - New Life
- Northern Ireland Statistics and Research Agency
- Patent Office
- Royal British Legion Small Business Advisory & Loan Scheme
- SFEDI - Small Firms Enterprise Development Initiative
- SmallBiz UK.com
- SmallBusiness.co.uk
- SmallBusinessAdvice.org.uk
- Social Economy Agency
- Startbusiness.co.uk
- StartInBusiness.co.uk
- StartingaBusinessinBritain.com
- Startups.co.uk

- Success4Business
- The-Bag-Lady.co.uk
- The-SME.co.uk
- Trade Partners UK
- TradeNetIreland Ltd
- Trading Standards Institute
- UK Business Incubation
- UK Online
- WhichFranchise.com.

INTELLECTUAL PROPERTY

- Intellectual Property UK
- Patent Office
- UUTech Ltd.

INWARDS INVESTMENT

- InvestNI.

LEGAL

- Law Society of Northern Ireland.

MARKETING

- Business Innovation Centres
- Mintel International Group Ltd
- TradeNetIreland Ltd.

MENTORING

- British Association of Women Entrepreneurs
- Institute of Business Advisers.

NETWORKING

- British Association of Women Entrepreneurs
- everywoman.co.uk
- EW-Network
- Federation of Small Businesses
- First Tuesday
- Home Business Alliance
- Institute for Small Business Affairs
- Institute of Directors
- PLATO Ireland
- UK Business Innovation.

POLICY

- Department of Agriculture & Rural Development (NORTHERN IRELAND)
- Department of Enterprise, Trade & Investment (NORTHERN IRELAND)
- Institute for Small Business Affairs
- InterTradeIreland
- Northern Ireland Executive
- Northern Ireland Office
- Small Business Service.

PUBLICATIONS

- Beermat Entrepreneur
- Better-business.co.uk
- Health & Safety Executive for Northern Ireland
- Oak Tree Press.

R&D

- Business Innovation Link
- Chartered Institute of Patent Agents
- UK Science Park Association.

REGULATOR & STANDARDS

- Companies Registry (NORTHERN IRELAND)
- Environment Agency
- Health & Safety Executive for Northern Ireland
- HM Customs & Excise
- Inland Revenue
- Investors in People
- Patent Office
- SFEDI - Small Firms Enterprise Development Initiative
- Trading Standards Institute.

SOCIAL ECONOMY

- School for Social Entrepreneurs
- Seo-Online.org.uk
- Social Economy Agency.

START-UP TRAINING

- Jobcentre Plus
- National Extension College
- Oak Tree Press
- Prince's Trust Northern Ireland.

TRAINING

- Business Innovation Centres
- Department for Employment & Learning (NORTHERN IRELAND)
- Ibis Associates
- Institute of Business Advisers
- Institute of Directors
- Institute of Leadership & Management
- Learn Direct for Business
- National Extension College
- Oak Tree Press
- PLATO Ireland
- School for Social Entrepreneurs
- SEED
- Social Economy Agency
- Trading Standards Institute.

WEBSITE

- Aurora Women's Network
- Better-business.co.uk
- Beyond Bricks Ecademy
- Bplans.org.uk
- Business Bureau UK

- BusinessInformationPoint.com
- ClearlyBusiness.co.uk
- eGrindstone.co.uk
- Everywoman.co.uk
- EW-Network
- FastLinkSolutions.co.uk
- Getfinance.co.uk
- Government Direct for Business
- Grantfinder
- HM Customs & Excise
- Inland Revenue
- Innovateur
- j4b.co.uk
- New Business – New Life
- Oak Tree Press
- SmallBiz UK.com
- SmallBusiness.co.uk
- SmallBusinessAdvice.org.uk
- Startbusiness.co.uk
- StartInBusiness.co.uk
- StartingaBusinessinBritain.com
- Startups.co.uk
- Success4Business
- The-Bag-Lady.co.uk
- The-SME.co.uk
- TradeNetIreland Ltd
- UK Online
- WhichFranchise.com.

WOMEN

- Aurora Women's Network
- British Association of Women Entrepreneurs
- Everywoman.co.uk
- EW-Network
- SEED
- The-Bag-Lady.co.uk.

YOUNG ENTERPRISE

- Prince's Trust Northern Ireland
- Shell LiveWIRE
- Young Enterprise Northern Ireland.

9

EU SUPPORT FOR START-UPS IN BRITAIN

Support from the European Union for start-ups and small businesses in Britain comes in two forms:

- Direct

- Indirect.

DIRECT ASSISTANCE

This is usually in the form of information and guidance through EU-funded agencies such as:

- Business Innovation Centres

- European Information Centres

- ICASS

- Innovation Relay Centres

- The European Commission's own offices.

INDIRECT ASSISTANCE

This is delivered indirectly through Government and other agencies, for example:

* Structural Funds, which support Government spending – information on these funds is available from the European Commission's offices.

Full information on the European Union and its support for enterprise in Britain, and across the EU generally, is available on the *Europa* website.

10

IMPLEMENTATION

OK! So you're ready to go – market research done, business plan drafted, finance and supports in place. But there are a few small hurdles that could still trip you.

You ought to consider each of the following and build them into your business plan:

- Bank account
- Legal structure
- Taxation
- Advisers
- Accounting systems
- Quality certification.

BANK ACCOUNT

At least one bank account is an essential for any business, however small. Don't be tempted to run your business through your own personal bank account 'until it gets off the ground'. That is a recipe for disaster. Open a separate bank account for your business as soon as (or before) you begin to trade.

A limited liability company needs to pass a resolution of the Board of Directors to open a bank account. The steps are usually (check with your bank for their specific requirements):

- Ask your bank manager for a copy of the form of resolution that the bank requires. This is called a Bank Mandate because it mandates (that is, authorises) the bank to carry out the instructions of the directors regarding the operation of the account.

- Hold a meeting of the directors of the company.

- Decide what instructions you want to give the bank regarding who is authorised to sign cheques on behalf of the company, and how often you want to receive statements.

- Propose the resolution in the form required by the bank – see the mandate form for the wording – and have it adopted by the directors at a formal Board meeting.

- Complete the mandate form. Usually this is in the format of a request to the bank to open an account, and certifies that the resolution, in the prescribed wording, was passed at a meeting of the directors held on the date noted.

- Get sample signatures from each of the people authorised to sign cheques on behalf of the company.

- Return the mandate form and sample signatures to your bank manager.

- Give the bank manager a copy of your company's Memorandum of Association and Articles of Association. These will be kept for the bank's files.

- Show the original of the company's Certificate of Incorporation to your bank manager. A copy of this will be taken for the manager's files and on the copy will be marked the fact that the original has been seen by the manager. You should not give the bank manager, the original Certificate of Incorporation. (The only exception to this is in the larger city branches where the documents needed to open your bank account go to the Securities department for checking. In this case, your bank manager should give you a receipt for the certificate and give you a date when you can return to collect it.)

- Have available some money to lodge to the new account.

- Decide the name in which you want the account to be opened.

Depending on the bank and branch, it may take a few days or a few weeks to clear all the paperwork associated with opening your company's bank account. Allow for this in your planning.

If you need immediate access to the funds you are lodging, your bank manager can usually arrange for temporary cheques to be made available while a chequebook is being printed.

LEGAL STRUCTURE

You have most likely already made a choice as to your legal structure (see **Chapter 2**). Now you need to implement it.

Setting Up as a Sole Trader

You automatically become a sole trader by starting up a business. Setting up as a sole trader needs almost nothing by way of legal formality. A further advantage of being a sole trader is that apart from normal tax returns, which every business must make, a sole trader is not required to make public any information on the business.

Setting Up as a Partnership

A partnership, essentially, is an agreement between two or more people to go into business together. It may be no more formal than a handshake or may run to a multi-page legal document. Whichever route you take, build the following points into your planning:

- In a partnership, each partner is liable for all the liabilities of the business. If the business fails, and your partner(s) abandon(s) you, you could be left to pay for everything out of your own pocket. Before entering a partnership, decide whether you trust your partner(s)-to-be with everything you own – because that's what you will be doing.

- If you write down nothing else, write down and have all the partners sign a document setting out how the business is to be financed, how profits and losses are to be shared, and what will happen if one of the partners decides to leave. These are important points. Failure to agree on them at an early stage can lead to difficulty later.

Note, however, that you can achieve limited liability in a partnership structure by incorporating as a limited liability partnership. Companies House offers useful guidance.

Forming a Limited Liability Company

A limited liability company is a legal entity separate from its shareholders. The shareholders are only liable, in the event of the business becoming unable to pay its debts, for any amount outstanding on their subscribed shareholdings.

The steps involved in forming a limited company are:

- Decide on a name for your company. (Note that there are some restrictions – see the Companies House guidance booklet 'Company Names'.)

- Define the purpose for which the company is being formed. This will make up the company's Objects clause.

- Prepare the Memorandum of Association, which states what the company has been set up to do, who the initial share-holders are and how much they have subscribed.

- Prepare the Articles of Association, which details the rules governing internal procedures of the company.

- Complete Form 10 (details of the first directors, secretary and registered office) and Form 12 (a statutory declaration of compliance with all the legal obligations relating to the formation of the company).

- Submit all these, with a cheque or draft for the formation fees, to *Companies House*.

The cost of forming a limited company depends on whether you do the work yourself or ask an accountant, solicitor, or company formation agent to do it for you. The standard Companies House fee is £20 (£80 for same day formation). Typically, using a professional is more expensive.

TAXATION

Businesses in the UK are subject to:

- **Income Tax** – Sole traders and partnerships on their profits

- **Corporation Tax** – Limited companies on their profits

- **Value Added Tax (VAT)** – All businesses with turnover over £55,000

- **National Insurance Contributions (NIC)** – All businesses with employees (including owner/directors).

Two agencies are involved:

- **Inland Revenue** – for Income Tax, Corporation Tax and National Insurance Contributions

- **HM Customs & Excise** – for VAT.

Registration for tax

It is your obligation to notify the Inland Revenue/HM Customs & Excise through your local tax office of the establishment of your business and to provide them with the information required to register your business for the relevant taxes.

Your starting point is to get a copy of the Inland Revenue/HM Customs & Excise *Starting Up in Business* pack by telephoning **08457 646 646**, contacting your local tax office (check the telephone directory), or through **www.inlandrevenue.gov.uk**.

You should also consider attending a Business Advice Open Day – telephone **0121 697 4065** for more information.

Corporation Tax

Limited liability companies pay Corporation Tax on the company's total profits, including any capital gains, for an accounting period – normally the period for which the company's accounts are prepared, though an accounting period cannot exceed 12 months.

A self-assessment system applies to companies. The company assesses its own liability to tax and pays it no later than nine months after the end of the accounting period. Payments can be made by cheque, GIRO, or electronically through the BACS or CHAPS systems. Interest will be charged if payments are made after their due date.

The company will also complete a Company Tax Return (CT600) and send it to the Inland Revenue with its accounts for the period.

The company's self-assessment is then complete, unless changes are made to the return by the company or the Inland Revenue query it. Inland Revenue queries some returns to check that they are correct or to understand better the figures in them.

The rates of Corporation Tax are:

• **Main Rate** – 30%, on profits over £1,500,000

- **Small Companies' Rate** – 19% on profits between £50,001 and £300,000

- **Starting Rate** – Nil on profits up to £10,000.

Marginal relief, which applies less than the full rate of the next tax band, applies to profits between £10,001 and £50,000 and between £300,001 and £1,500,000.

You should read *A general guide to Corporation Tax Self-Assessment* (CTSA/BK4), available from your local tax office or from the Inland Revenue web-site.

Income Tax

Income tax is payable by self-employed individuals on income earned in the tax year – that is, on annual profits or gains from an individual's trade, profession or vocation and on other income, such as investment income, rental income etc.

As soon as you start business as a self-employed person, you must complete Form CWF1, *Notification of Self-employment* and send it to the Inland Revenue National Insurance Contributions Office. This office will then tell:

- Your local tax office

- HM Customs & Excise (if your turnover is more than £55,000 in a 12-month period, you must register for VAT – see below)

- Your Job Centre, if you are registered with one.

Your tax office requires a return of your business income and expenses in a standard format. You do not need to prepare separate accounts, although you may find that your bank wants to see formal accounts anyway.

Income tax is calculated on a 12-month basis, for a year running from 6 April to the following 5 April.

In April, you will receive a tax return, asking you for the information needed to calculate your tax bill for the year. If you can calculate the bill yourself (the return explains how), you must send back the return by 31 January following. Alternatively, you can ask the Inland Revenue to calculate the tax bill, based on the information on your return. In this case, you must send back your return before 30 September.

In your second and later years in business, you must make two payments on account against your tax bill each year. These payments are due on 31 January (during the relevant tax year to 5 April) and 31 July (just after its end). The final payment of your tax bill must be made by 31 January following the end of the tax year.

Calculating taxable profits

Taxable profits are calculated by deducting allowable business expenses from turnover. Turnover is the gross amount of income earned by a business before deducting any business expenses – the total amounts from sale of goods or provision of services. If a business is registered for VAT, the turnover figure should exclude VAT.

Business expenses are normally referred to as revenue expenditure, which covers day-to-day running costs (exclusive of VAT, if the business is registered for VAT), including:

- Purchase of goods for resale

- Wages, rent, rates, repairs, lighting, heating etc

- Running costs of vehicles or machinery used in the business

- Accountancy and audit fees

- Interest paid on any monies borrowed to finance business expenses/items

- Lease payments on vehicles or machinery used in the business.

Some expenses cannot be claimed as revenue expenditure, including:

- Any expense, not wholly and exclusively paid for the purposes of the trade or profession

- Any private or domestic expenditure

- Business entertainment expenditure – the provision of accommodation, food, drink or any other form of hospitality

- Expenditure of a capital nature.

For expenditure relating to both business and private use, only that part relating to the business will be allowed.

Expenditure is regarded as 'capital' if it has been spent on acquiring or altering assets that are of lasting use in the business – for example, buying or altering business premises. Capital expenditure cannot be deducted in arriving at the taxable profit. However, capital allowances may be claimed on capital expenditure incurred on items such as office equipment, business plant and machinery, to take account of wear and tear on these items.

To arrive at the correct taxable income, the net profit should be calculated and any allowances and relief entitlements deducted.

Self-employed National Insurance Contributions

Self-employed people pay National Insurance Contributions in two classes: Class 2 and Class 4 (on profits above a certain level).

PAYE & National Insurance Contributions

When you employ someone in your business, you should immediately tell your local tax office. They will send you a *New Employer's Starter Pack* and tell the local Business Support Team, which provides payroll support to employers in their area.

The Pay As You Earn (PAYE) system operates on the basis that an employer deducts tax at a specified rate from an employee's pay. The system is designed so that, as far as is possible, the correct amount of tax is deducted from an employee's pay to meet his/her tax liability for the year. To achieve this, PAYE is normally computed on a cumulative basis, from the beginning of the tax year to the date on which a payment is being made.

In addition to deducting PAYE, employers are also obliged to deduct National Insurance Contributions (NIC) from employees.

You must:

- Work out employees' PAYE and NIC each pay day

- Pay this amount to the Inland Revenue monthly

- Tell your local tax office at the end of each tax year how much each employee has earned and what PAYE and NIC you have deducted.

Your local Inland Revenue Business Support Team will advise you on the details.

Value Added Tax

Value Added Tax (VAT) is a consumer tax collected by VAT-registered traders on their supplies of taxable goods and services in the course of business and by Customs & Excise on imports from outside the EU.

Each trader pays VAT on goods and services acquired for the business and charges VAT on goods and services supplied by the business. The amount by which VAT charged exceeds VAT paid must be paid to HM Customs & Excise.

If the amount of VAT paid exceeds the VAT charged, you will get a refund. This ensures that VAT is paid by the ultimate customer and not by the business.

You must register for VAT if your turnover for a 12-month period exceeds £55,000 (this amount is reviewed annually). Traders whose turnover is below this limit are not obliged to register for VAT but may do so if they wish. You should only do so on your accountant's advice.

The current rate of VAT is 17.5%, though some goods and services are zero rated or taxed at a reduced rate of 5%.

The Annual Accounting Scheme allows you to pay monthly direct debits and send in a single VAT return at the end of the year. The Cash Accounting Scheme lets you account for VAT on the basis of cash paid and received, rather than invoices issued and received. You should take advice from your accountant before registering for either of these schemes. Both schemes are subject to maximum turnover limits, currently £600,000.

Record-keeping

The Inland Revenue requires all businesses to keep 'sufficient' records of transactions to allow the correct tax to be calculated. You must keep:

- Details of all receipts and expenses incurred in the course of your business and of what they relate to

- Details of all sales and purchases made in the course of the trade, if you deal in goods

- All other supporting documents.

The Inland Revenue publishes a number of guides (available on its web-site) that provide guidance in this area. Most businesses set up as a limited liability company will be required by law to keep certain records in order to prepare accounts. In most cases, the Companies Acts requirements are the same as the Inland Revenue's – except that the Inland Revenue requires records to be kept for six years, while the Companies Acts only requires private limited companies to keep records for three years. Note that alternatives to the original documents – for example, optical images, etc - are usually acceptable.

Returns

For each of the taxes, you are required to supply the Revenue Commissioners with specific information on or by specific dates. These are called 'returns' and there are severe penalties for late submission or not submitting returns at all.

Information and assistance

Comprehensive guides to all aspects of business taxation, including a 'Starting Your Own Business?' guide, may be obtained from any tax office or the Inland Revenue's web-site (**www.inlandrevenue.gov.uk**). Your accountant will also provide advice.

Taxpayers' Charter

It's not all one way, however. The Inland Revenue has issued a *Taxpayers' Charter*, which sets out your rights as a taxpayer. Ask at your local tax office for a copy.

On-line Services

The Inland Revenue is increasingly moving on-line. Not only are all forms and publications available on their web-site but increasingly taxpayers can make returns and payments on-line too.

Talk to an accountant

Because tax regulations are becoming increasingly complicated, it is worth talking to an accountant about your specific situation and needs.

ADVISERS

As you start in business, you need two key advisers: an accountant and a solicitor. In the pressures of setting up your new business, there will be a temptation to avoid finding either of these two. Not doing so saves you time and possibly money, both of which are important in a start-up situation. But it could cost you dearly later on.

The reasons for choosing a financial and a legal adviser at the start are:

- Their experience and expertise in dealing with other start-ups may save you hours of time and hundreds, or even thousands, of pounds. If they are the right advisers for you, they will be prepared to assist your enterprise with timely and constructive advice – take it and use it!

- With luck, you will never find yourself in a situation where you need to be bailed out of a difficult situation, but if you do, it's better to have your advisers on your team already than have to start looking for them with the millstone of your problem around your neck.

In choosing advisers, look for:

- Membership of the appropriate professional body. This is your guarantee of quality of work and source of redress, should the need ever arise

- Experience in the type of business or at least in the business area in which you intend to operate. You want to learn from your advisers' experience, not spend your time teaching them about your business

- Adequate resources to meet your needs. What is adequate will depend on you, but don't choose a one-man band if you expect a limitless range of expertise. There is only so much one person can be expert in. Ask about the advisers' hours of business (actual hours, not published hours). Can you

telephone them at seven o'clock on a Sunday night? What
happens when they go on holidays?

* People you can trust and work easily with. If you can't trust
  your advisers with your most confidential information, you
  shouldn't have them on your team. Find someone else.

Choosing an Accountant

If your business is set up as a limited liability company, and has
a turnover in excess of £1 million, your accountant will have one
primary task: to carry out the annual audit. This is a statutory
inspection of the company's accounting records, which results
in a formal set of accounts and an audit report. Below the £1
million threshold, companies are not required to have their
accounts audited, although they may do so if they wish.

Even if you do not need (or want) an audit, there are benefits
in using an accountant to help you manage your finances.

Many accountants provide advice and assistance in taking a
business concept from viability assessment through to the
production stage and also in obtaining assistance from
Government and other support organisations.

If you do not know a suitable accountant, check the *Yellow
Pages* or contact one of the accounting bodies listed in the
Directory.

An initial meeting between a potential entrepreneur and the
accountant is usually free and is used to gather information
about the promoter and the business proposal. Based on the
information available, appropriate action to advance the
project will be agreed. Where further information is required, a
structured feasibility study is carried out, embracing key
aspects such as products, markets, competitors, technology,
funding etc. A fee should be agreed before work starts. If the
proposal is viable, the accountant will assist in the preparation
of a comprehensive business plan, at a further agreed cost.
They will make application for grants appropriate to the project

and assist in raising finance from banks or private investors. They may also help to obtain commercial partners.

Choosing a Solicitor

Unlike an accountant, a solicitor has no statutory duties in relation to a company. You will, however, need a solicitor for the following:

- To sign a statutory declaration when you are forming your company.

- To check out the lease of any premises you decide to buy or rent.

- To prepare employment contracts for you and your staff.

- To draft or review contracts that you enter into with customers or suppliers.

In addition, from time to time, you may require advice on legal issues.

If you do not know a suitable solicitor, look in the *Yellow Pages* or contact one of the organisations listed in the **Directory**.

ACCOUNTING SYSTEMS

Accounts systems provide a record of all the income and outgoings of a business and produce the basic information for the end-of-year accounts and for management information.

In a manual system, you may need some or all of the following (in varying levels of detail, depending on the size and complexity of your business – your accountant will advise. See also the Inland Revenue's requirements for record-keeping):

- Cash book

- Petty-cash book

- Purchase day book

- Purchase ledger

- Sales day book

- Sales ledger

- Control accounts

- Wages book/deduction sheets

- Register of fixed assets

- Nominal ledger

- System for ordering goods/dealing with purchase invoices

- System for dealing with customers' orders, sales invoices

- Credit control procedures

- Control of workforce and hours worked

- Stock control procedures

- System for regular management information

- Adequate control procedures by management over employees.

You can also use a computerised accounting system (again, your accountant will advise).

Your accountant will also advise you on a system for filing and retrieving documents. You also need to consider the flow of documents and information around the business – for example, how a customer order is processed so that the goods are sent out, an invoice generated and payment received.

Whether manual or computerised, there are three simple aids that you should use to help you in the financial control of your business. These are:

- Bank balance book

- Still-to-be-received file

- Still-to-be-paid file.

The bank balance book does exactly what its name suggests – it tells you what your bank balance is. You need five columns – for the date, for the transaction detail (cheque or lodgement will do), for lodgements, for cheques and other withdrawals, and for the balance. If every transaction with your bank is written into this book *when it happens,* you will always know your correct bank balance. The little effort that it takes to keep this book up to date will be more than repaid as it keeps you out of trouble.

Cash flow is important for any business. If you sell goods on credit, you will probably find that you spend a great deal of time chasing debtors, trying to collect money. A 'still-to-be-received' file helps you by providing all the information you need on outstanding debts. Just put a copy of every invoice into the file when you issue it, and take the copy out when it is paid – then every invoice in the file represents an unpaid debt, money due to you. You can list them out, total them up, cry over them – whatever takes your fancy – but you have accurate information on which to do so.

The 'still-to-be-paid' file works in the opposite way – it reminds you of money you owe. Put a copy of every invoice you receive into it and take it out when you pay it (send the copy with your cheque so that your creditor knows which invoice you are paying!) – and what's left is what you owe. So, when you get a telephone call saying that such and such an invoice is due for payment or overdue, you can check it out immediately.

QUALITY CERTIFICATION

For some businesses in particular, and increasingly for all businesses, some form of quality certification is becoming essential. Schemes such as ISO 9000 are the norm among high-tech companies and are a minimum requirement to supply many larger companies.

ISO 9000 is a standard for quality management systems, covering every stage of the production process – procurement, incoming materials, production performance, final inspection, and delivery. To implement ISO 9000 (or any quality standard):

- Management has to define clearly what is needed.

- The message must reach staff so that everybody knows what they have to do and how to do it.

- The right equipment, processes and tools must be there to do the job.

- The right information must reach the appropriate people at the right time.

- There must be a system of management and control.

For further information, read *ISO 9000*, by Brian Rothery (2nd edition, Gower, ISBN 0-566-07402-8).

Even if your business's involvement in quality certification stems purely from a supplier-imposed requirement, keep two things firmly in mind:

- Quality is an attitude of mind, a way of working, not just mindless compliance with written procedures. Most quality schemes involve the recording of operational procedures, together with systems to audit compliance. Make sure that compliance with the system does not become the end, rather than quality itself.

- Quality involves a cost and any investment in quality systems must be justified like any other business expense. Investing in quality for its own sake may be very noble, but it's not good business.

DIRECTORY OF SOURCES OF SUPPORT

The aims of this directory are:

- To highlight the many sources of assistance available to start-up and small/medium-sized enterprises in Britain

- To direct readers to sources appropriate to their needs.

The directory is arranged alphabetically by organisation, with full contact details (address, telephone, fax, e-mail, website and contact name) for each, where possible.

Each entry summarises the assistance provided by the organisation. Where an organisation has links with other organisations listed in the directory, these are shown in the text thus: *Other Organisation*.

The categories under which the organisations are shown in **Chapters 5** (England), **6** (Scotland), **7** (Wales) and **8** (Northern Ireland) are shown thus **[Category]**. References to **[EU Support]** are to **Chapter 9**.

All the information has been checked before publication but, of course, it is subject to change. Contact the organisations directly for the most up to date position.

3i GROUP PLC

91 Waterloo Road, London SE1 8XP
T: 0207 928 3131 F: 0207 928 0058
E: london@3i.com (London Head Office) W: www.3i.com
[Equity]
3i provides venture capital and private equity for start-ups with high
growth potential and strong management.

ABBEY NATIONAL

Abbey National House, 2 Triton Square, Regent's Place,
London NW1 3AN
T: 0845 6070 666
W: www.anbusiness.com
[Debt]
Traditionally a mortgage provider, Abbey National also offers
business banking services.

ADVANTAGE WEST MIDLANDS
(REGIONAL DEVELOPMENT AGENCY FOR THE WEST MIDLANDS)

3 Priestley Wharf, Holt Street, Aston Science Park,
Birmingham B7 4BN
T: 0121 380 3500 F: 0121 380 3501
E: info@advantagewm.co.uk W: www.advantagewm.co.uk
**[Community & Rural Development; Enterprise Support; Grants;
Incubator; Inwards Investment; Policy]**
One of the nine *Regional Development Agencies* established by the
Government in 1999/2000 to promote the sustainable economic
development of the regions. Advantage West Midlands works in
partnership with national and local organisations as a regional
champion, securing funding and investment, and in bringing other
organisations together to deliver actions of regional significance -
such as the Advantage Technology Fund, or the Regeneration Zones,
High Technology Corridors and Cluster Development. It also
provides investment to support regeneration, inward investment,
business growth and skills development programmes in the region.
See also *West Midlands Finance*.

AFRICAN CARIBBEAN BUSINESS FORUM

c/o Birmingham Chamber of Commerce & Industry, Chamber House,
75 Harborne Road, Edgbaston, Birmingham B15 3DH
T: 0121 6070 8090 F: 0121 607 9899
E: info@birmingham.businesslink.co.uk
W: www.birmingham-chamber.net
[Information; Minorities & Disabilities; Policy]
Birmingham-based, and working with key strategic partners, ACBF
supports the design, development and delivery of initiatives relevant
to Afro-Caribbean entrepreneurs.

ALLIANCE & LEICESTER BUSINESS BANKING

Bridle Road, Bootle, Merseyside GIR 0AA
T: 0800 587 0800
W: www.mybusinessbank.co.uk
[Debt]
Offers to start-ups include 12 months free banking, free internet
banking, dedicated start-up managers and free interactive business
planning software.

ALLIED IRISH BANK (GB)

Bankcentre, Belmont Road, Uxbridge, Middlesex UB8 1SA
T: 01895 272222
E: aibgb@aib.ie W: www.aibgb.co.uk
[Debt]
Allied Irish Bank provides a full range of banking services throughout
the UK. See also *First Trust Bank* for Northern Ireland.

APAX PARTNERS LTD

15 Portland Place, London, W1B 1PT
T: 0207 872 6300 F: 0207 636 6475
E: Suzanne.Epstein@apax.com W: www.apax.com
[Equity]
An international venture capital company.

ASIAN BUSINESS FORUM

c/o Birmingham Chamber of Commerce & Industry, Chamber House,
75 Harborne Road, Edgbaston, Birmingham B15 3DH
T: 0121 6070 8090 F: 0121 607 9899
E: info@birmingham.businesslink.co.uk
W: www.birmingham-chamber.net.
[Information; Minorities & Disabilities; Policy]
Birmingham-based, ABF is a strategic think-tank of local business
leaders, whose role is to provide advice and guidance to *The Institute
of Asian Businesses*, Asian Business Consortium, Birmingham Asian
Business Association (BABA) and *Business Link Birmingham*.

ASSOCIATION OF BRITISH CREDIT UNIONS LTD

Holyoake House, Hanover Street, Manchester M60 0AS
T: 0161 832 3694 F: 0161 832 3706
E: info@abcul.org W: www.abcul.org
[Debt]
ABCUL is the main trade association for credit unions in England,
Scotland and Wales. Its website offers a search facility to find credit
unions across the UK.

ASSOCIATION OF CHARTERED CERTIFIED ACCOUNTANTS

29 Lincoln's Inn Fields, London WC2A 3EE
T: 0207 396 7000 F: 0207 396 7070
E: info@accaglobal.com W: www.acca.org.uk
[Accountants]
ACCA is one of the accountancy bodies whose members are
permitted to audit company accounts. If you're looking for an
accountant, ACCA can direct you to one of its members.

AURORA WOMEN'S NETWORK

Prospect House, 80-110 New Oxford Street, London WC1A 1HB
T: 0207 908 8002 F: 0709 229 7844
E: admin@auroravoice.com W: www.busygirl.com
[Information; Networking; Website; Women]
Formerly Busygirl, Aurora is a free membership network for the
economic advancement of corporate and entrepreneurial women.

BANK OF IRELAND NORTHERN IRELAND

54 Donegall Place, Belfast BT1 5BX
T: 028 9023 4334
W: www.bankofireland.co.uk
[Debt]
Bank of Ireland in Northern Ireland offers a full range of banking
services to start-ups and small businesses.

BANK OF IRELAND UK

36 Queen Street, London EC4R 1HJ
T: 0207 236 2000
E: boigb.web@boiuk.com W: www.bank-of-ireland.co.uk
[Debt]
Bank of Ireland UK offers a full range of banking services to start-ups
and small businesses, with branches throughout the UK.

BANK OF SCOTLAND LTD

Business Banking eCommerce, 1st Floor, New Uberior House,
11 Earl Grey Street, Edinburgh EH3 9BN
T: 0845 608 0039
W: www.bankofscotland.co.uk
[Debt]
Offers a full range of banking services for small businesses – details at
www.bankofscotland.co.uk/business/startup/lgstarting/index.html.

BARCLAYS BANK

54 Lombard Street, London EC3P 3AH
W: www.barclays.co.uk
[Debt]
Barclays currently helps over 70,000 start-ups each year and provides
banking services to over 350,000 small businesses in the UK. See also
ClearlyBusiness.co.uk.

BECAUSEYOUCAN.COM

W: www.becauseyoucan.com
[Information; Website]
This website is part of the Entrepreneurial Action Plan from the *Welsh
Development Agency*, aimed at stimulating and encouraging
entrepreneurship in Wales.

BEERMAT ENTREPRENEUR

W: www.beermatentrepreneur.com
[Information; Publications]
Based on the best-selling book of the same name, Beermat
Entrepreneur now offers consultancy to start-ups and growing
companies. See also *Beyond Bricks Ecademy*.

BELFAST FIRST STOP BUSINESS SHOP

14 Wellington Place, Belfast, BT1 6GE
T: 028 9027 8399 F: 028 9027 8398
E: info@firststopshop.co.uk W: www.firststopshop.co.uk
[Information]
The First Stop Business Shop co-ordinates an information and
'signposting' service for existing and potential businesses.

BETHANY GROUP

St. Silas House, 18 Moore Street, Sheffield S3 7UW
T: 0114 7281 5677 F: 0114 2815657
E: Sharon@bethanygroup.net W: www.bethanygroup.co.uk
[Start-Up Training]
Bethany's Business Start Up Programmes provide a pro-active,
dynamic service incorporating the use of modern technology, to
stimulate enterprise activity. See also *DHP Enterprise* and *DHP
Scotland*.

BETTER-BUSINESS.CO.UK

Active Information Ltd, Cribau Mill, Chepstow NP16 6LN, Wales
T: 0845 458 9485 F: 01291 641777
E: info@better-business.co.uk W: www.better-business.co.uk
[Information; Publications; Website]
This website is based on the journal of the same name.

BEYOND BRICKS ECADEMY

W: www.beyondbricks.com
[Information; Website]
Launched as part of the Internet Mentoring Initiative by DTI, Beyond
Bricks Ecademy is now operated by Ecademy, *SmallBiz UK* and the
Beermat Entrepreneur, as a community for small businesses.

BioTech-Scotland

W: www.biotech-scotland.org
[Information; R&D]
The Biotech Scotland website provides news and information from the Scottish biotech community. Biotech Scotland is a marketing initiative of the *Scottish Enterprise Network* Biotechnology Group.

BizWise.co.uk

W: www.bizwise.co.uk
[Information; Website]
BizWise provides subscribers with online guidance and telephone support, including briefings, checklists and weekly newsletters.

Black Training & Enterprise Group

Regent's Wharf, 8 All Saints Street, London N1 9RL
T: 0207 713 6161 F: 0207 837 0269
E: bteg@btinternet.com W: www.bteg.co.uk
[Minorities & Disabilities; Policy]
BTEG is a national organisation working to improve opportunities in black communities.

Bplans.org.uk

W: www.bplans.org.uk
[Business Plans; Website]
Bplans.org.uk contains the largest single collection of free sample business plans online. In addition, Bplans.org.uk includes practical advice on planning. See also *Palo Alto Software*.

BRIDGES COMMUNITY VENTURES LTD

1 Craven Hill, London W2 3EN
T: 0207 262 5566 F: 0207 262 6389
E: info@bridgesventures.com W: www.bridgesventures.com
[**Community & Rural Development**]
Bridges Community Ventures manages the Community Development
Venture Fund, more commonly known as the Bridges Fund, which
provides venture capital to viable small and medium-sized
enterprises, capable of substantial growth and located in the more
disadvantaged communities of England. Applicants must demonstrate
high growth potential, a viable business plan and have strong
economic links to the community involved.

BRISTOL & WEST PLC

One Temple Back East, Temple Quay, Bristol BS1 6DX
T: 0117 979 2222 F: 0117 929 3787
W: www.bristol-west.co.uk
[**Debt**]
Owned by *Bank of Ireland*, and traditionally a mortgage provider,
Bristol & West also offers professional and corporate banking.

BRITISH ASSOCIATION OF WOMEN ENTREPRENEURS

Suite F, 123-125 Gloucester Place, London W1H 3PJ
T: 0207 935 0085 F: 0207 486 6016
E: president@bawe-uk.org W: www.bawe-uk.org
[**Information; Mentoring; Networking; Women**]
BAWE is a non-profit professional organisation for UK-based women
business-owners, affiliated to the world association of women
business-owners, Les Femmes Chefs d'Entreprises Mondiales.

BRITISH CHAMBERS OF COMMERCE

1st Floor, 65 Petty France, St James's Park, London SW1H 9EU
T: 0207 654 5800 F: 0207 654 5819
E: info@britishchambers.org.uk W: www.chamberonline.co.uk
[**Information; Networking; Training**]
The British Chambers of Commerce is a national network of local,
independent, non-profit making and non party-political organisations,
funded by membership subscriptions. Members benefit from
business training, information resources, networking and savings on
essential overheads. BCC is also part of the global network of
Chambers of Commerce.

Chambers in the UK include:

- Aberdeen and Grampian Chamber of Commerce
- Ashford (Kent) Chamber of Commerce, Industry & Enterprise Ltd
- Barnsley Chamber of Commerce & Industry
- Bedfordshire & Luton Chamber of Commerce
- Birmingham Chamber of Commerce & Industry
- Black Country Chamber of Commerce
- Bolton & Bury Chamber of Commerce Training & Enterprise
- Bradford Chamber of Commerce
- Bristol Chamber of Commerce & Initiative
- Cambridge & District Chamber of Commerce & Industry
- Cardiff Chamber of Commerce & Industry
- Central & West Lancashire Chamber of Commerce & Industry
- Chester, Ellesmere Port & North Wales Chamber of Commerce & Industry
- Coventry & Warwickshire Chamber of Commerce, Training & Enterprise
- Doncaster Chamber of Commerce & Enterprise
- Dorset Chamber of Commerce & Industry
- Dundee & Tayside Chamber of Commerce & Industry
- East Lancashire Chamber of Commerce & Industry
- Edinburgh Chamber of Commerce & Enterprise
- Essex Chamber of Commerce
- Fife Chamber of Commerce
- Glasgow Chamber of Commerce
- Herefordshire & Worcesteshire Chamber of Commerce
- Hertfordshire Chamber of Commerce & Industry
- Hull & Humber Chamber of Commerce Industry & Shipping
- Isle of Wight Chamber of Commerce
- Leeds Chamber of Commerce
- Leicestershire Chamber of Commerce & Industry
- Lincolnshire Chamber of Commerce & Industry
- Liverpool Chamber of Commerce & Industry
- London Chamber of Commerce & Industry
- Maidstone & Mid-Kent Chamber of Commerce
- Manchester Chamber of Commerce & Industry
- Milton Keynes & North Bucks Chamber of Commerce, Training & Enterprise

- Norfolk Chamber of Commerce & Industry
- North Derbyshire Chamber of Commerce & Industry
- North East Chamber of Commerce, Trade & Industry
- North Hampshire Chamber of Commerce, Trade & Industry
- North Staffordshire Chamber of Commerce & Industry
- Northamptonshire Chamber of Commerce, Training & Enterprise
- Northern Ireland Chamber of Commerce & Industry
- Nottinghamshire Chamber of Commerce
- Oldham Chamber of Commerce, Training & Enterprise
- Portsmouth & South East Hampshire Chamber of Commerce & Industry
- Rochdale Borough Chamber of Commerce, Training & Enterprise
- Rotherham Chamber of Commerce, Training & Enterprise
- Sheffield Chamber of Commerce & Industry
- Shepway Chamber of Commerce & Industry
- Shropshire Chamber of Commerce, Training & Enterprise
- South Cheshire Chamber of Commerce & Industry
- Southampton & Fareham Chamber of Commerce & Industry
- Southern Derbyshire Chamber of Commerce, Training & Enterprise
- Southern Staffordshire Chamber of Commerce & Industry
- St Helens Chamber
- Suffolk Chamber of Commerce Industry & Shipping Incorporated
- Surrey Chambers of Commerce
- Sussex Chamber of Commerce, Training & Enterprise (see Sussex Enterprise)
- Swindon Chamber of Commerce & Industry
- Thames Valley Chamber of Commerce
- Warrington Chamber of Commerce & Industry
- West Kent Chamber of Commerce & Industry
- Wigan Chamber of Commerce, Training & Enterprise
- York & North Yorkshire Chamber of Commerce.

BRITISH FRANCHISE ASSOCIATION

Thames View, Newtown Road, Henley-on-Thames, Oxon. RG9 1HG
T: 01491 578050 F: 01491 573517
E: mailroom@british-franchise.org.uk W: www.british-franchise.org
[Franchises]
This website provides information on franchising, as well as a list of
BFA members, all of whom are vetted against a code of business
practice. See also *WhichFranchise.com*.

BRITISH VENTURE CAPITAL ASSOCIATION

3 Clements Inn, London WC2A 2AZ
T: 0207 025 2950 F: 0207 025 2951
E: bvca@bvca.co.uk W: www.bvca.co.uk
[Equity]
The BVCA represents private equity and venture capital in the UK. Its
annual Directory of Members lists private equity firms and their
contact details and identifies their investment preferences (the
minimum and maximum amounts, financing stage, industry sector and
location) – details are also available on the BVCA website.

BUSINESS BUREAU UK

E: enquiries@businessbureau-uk.co.uk
W: www.businessbureau-uk.co.uk
[Information; Website]
A small business information resource online.

BUSINESS CONNECT WALES

Welsh Development Agency, Plas Glyndwr, Kingsway,
Cardiff CF10 3AH
T: 0845 796 9798 F: 029 2064 0031
E: executive@businessconnect.org.uk
W: www.businessconnect.org.uk
[Information; Website]
Business Connect Wales is an alliance of agencies, managed by the
Welsh Development Agency, that provides information, advice and
assistance to small and medium sized businesses in Wales, through a
website, telephone support and 32 centres across Wales:

- Aberystwyth
- Ammanford
- Anglesey
- Bangor
- Barry
- Brecon

- Bridgend
- Caernarfon
- Cardiff
- Cardigan
- Cwmbran (2)
- Dolegllau
- Lampeter
- Llandrindod Wells
- Llandudno Junction
- Merthyr Tydfil
- Mold
- Neath

- Newport
- Pembroke
- Penrhyndeudraeth
- Pontypridd
- Pwlheli
- Rhyl
- Ruthin
- Trawsffordd
- Tredegar
- Welshpool
- Wrexham (2)
- Ystrad Mynach.

BUSINESS INFORMATION SOURCE IN HIGHLAND SCOTLAND

Cowan House, Inverness Retail and Business Park, Inverness IV2 7GF
T: 01463 234171 F: 01463 244469
E: hie.general@hient.co.uk W: www.hie.co.uk
[Information; Website]
The Business Information Source is provided by *Highlands & Islands Enterprise*, as a network of Business Information Officers in Local Enterprise Companies to answer business enquiries. There is also a useful website.

BUSINESS INNOVATION CENTRES

W: www.ebn.be
[Equity; EU Support; Incubator; Information; Marketing; Training]
The Business Innovation Centres encourage and foster innovation in new or existing businesses, through services directed at the development of new ideas and their conversion into real business projects. There are 11 BICs in the UK in:

- Birmingham
- Cambridge
- Canterbury
- Chesterfield
- Coventry
- Derry

- London
- Manchester
- Nottingham
- Stafford
- Sunderland.

BUSINESS INNOVATION LINK

PO Box 838, Belfast BT5 7UW
T: 028 9041 9970 F: 028 9041 9970
[Grants; R&D]
Business Innovation Link is intended for the inventor or individual with
a good product idea who is seeking technical advice and financial
support towards product design and development. It assesses the
idea, the degree of product innovation, and the likely commercial
potential of the product. Financial assistance, up to £4,000, towards
the costs of a prototype may be available.

BUSINESS LINK

T: 0800 600 9006
W: www.businesslink.org
[Information; Website]
Business Link is the national business advice service. It provides
information for start-ups and small businesses, as well as access to a
network of business support organisations. Its website provides
factsheets, frequently asked questions and case studies.
There are Business Links across England, including:

- Bedfordshire & Luton
- Berkshire & Wiltshire
- Birmingham & Solihull
- Black Country
- Cambridgeshire
- Cheshire & Warrington
- County Durham
- Coventry & Warwickshire
- Cumbria
- Derbyshire
- Devon & Cornwall
- East Lancashire
- Essex
- Gloucestershire
- Greater Merseyside
- Hereford & Worcestershire
- Hertfordshire
- Humber
- Kent
- Leicestershire
- Lincolnshire & Rutland
- London
- Manchester
- Milton Keynes, Oxford & Buckinghamshire
- Norfolk
- North & Western Lancashire
- North Manchester
- Northamptonshire
- Northumberland
- Nottinghamshire
- Shropshire
- Somerset
- South Yorkshire
- Staffordshire
- Suffolk
- Surrey
- Sussex

- Tees Valley
- Tyne & Wear
- Wessex (Hampshire, Isle of Wight & Dorset)
- West
- West Yorkshire
- York & North Yorkshire.

BUSINESS MENTORING SCOTLAND

Bute Court, St. Andrews Drive, Glasgow Airport, PA3 2SW
T: 0845 609 6622
E: info@businessmentoringscotland.org
W: www.businessmentoringscotland.org
[Mentoring]
Scottish Enterprise Network's Business Mentoring Scotland programme brings successful business people into contact with growing businesses. The mentoring programme is delivered across Scotland by the *Scottish Chambers of Commerce* on behalf of the *Small Business Gateway* and *Highlands & Islands Enterprise*.

BUSINESS VOLUNTEER MENTORING ASSOCIATION

Contact via *National Federation of Enterprise Agencies*.
[Mentoring]
BVMA, which is managed by the *National Federation of Enterprise Agencies*, offers free mentoring advice from volunteers drawn from the business community.

BUSINESSINFORMATIONPOINT.COM

Strand House, 20 Strand Road, Derry BT48 7AB
T: 028 7126 3297 F: 028 7126 0302
E: info@businessinformationpoint.com
W: www.businessinformationpoint.com
[Information; Website]
This is a one-stop shop online for business information on Northern Ireland.

Capital Fund

London Fund Managers, 90 Long Acre, Covent Garden,
London WC2E 9RZ
T: 0207 849 3025 F: 0207 849 3026
E: info@thecapitalfund.co.uk W: www.thecapitalfund.co.uk
[Equity]
A new (2003) venture capital fund that invests in fast-growing, small
and medium enterprises in Greater London.

Chartered Institute of Management Accountants

26 Chapter Street, London SW1P 4NP
T: 0207 663 5441 F: 0207 663 5442
W: www.cimaglobal.com
[Accountants; Consultants]
While CIMA members may not audit companies' accounts, they can
assist businesses in a wide variety of ways as accountants and
consultants.

Chartered Institute of Patent Agents

Staple Inn Buildings, High Holborn, London WC1V 7PZ
Tel: 0207 405 9450 F: 0207 430 0471
E: mail@cipa.org.uk W: www.cipa.org.uk
[R&D]
CIPA is the professional body for patent attorneys. Its website offers a
directory of members, as well as information on protecting
innovation.

ClearlyBusiness.co.uk

1st floor, Gilray House, 146 - 150 City Road, London EC1V 2NL
T: 0845 601 5962
E: whatdoyouthink@clearlybusiness.com
W: www.clearlybusiness.co.uk
[Information; Website]
This website is backed by *Barclays Bank* and provides registered
users with a wide range of information for start-up and small
businesses. ClearlyBusiness offers the ClearlyBookkeeping package
and has recently launched ClearlyStartup, a CD-based resource pack.

CLYDESDALE BANK PLC

30 St Vincent Place, Glasgow, G1 2HL
T: 0141 951 7000 F: 0141 223 2443
W: www.clydesdalebank.co.uk
[Debt]
Clydesdale Bank is a member of the National Australia Bank Group,
which includes *National Irish Bank Limited*, *Northern Bank Limited*, and
Yorkshire Bank PLC. It offers a full range of banking services to small
businesses, through its branches across Scotland.

COMMUNITY ACTION NETWORK

The CAN Centre, The Mezzanine Floor, Elizabeth House,
39 York Road, London, SE1 7NQ
T: 0207 401 5310 F: 0207 401 5311
E: canhq@can-online.org.uk W: www.can-online.org.uk
[Community & Rural Development; Social Economy]
CAN is a mutual learning and support network for social
entrepreneurs. See also *SEO-Online.org.uk*.

COMPANIES HOUSE

Crown Way, Maindy, Cardiff CF4 3UZ
T: 01222 380801 F: 01222 380900
E: nbarnes@companieshouse.gov.uk
W: www.companieshouse.gov.uk
[Information; Regulator & Standards]
For registration and information about company formation. Offices in
Birmingham, Cardiff, Edinburgh, Leeds, London and Manchester. See
also *Companies Registry* (Northern Ireland).

COMPANIES REGISTRY (Northern Ireland)

64 Chichester Street, Belfast BT1 4JX
T: 028 9023 4488 F: 028 9054 4888
E: info.companiesregistry@detini.gov.uk
W: www.detini.gov.uk/registry/index.htm
[Information; Regulator & Standards]
For registration and information about company formation. See also
Companies House.

CONFEDERATION OF BRITISH BUSINESS

Centre Point, 103 New Oxford Street, London WC1A 1DU
T: 0207 395 8247 F: 0207 240 1578
W: www.cbi.org.uk
[Networking]
The CBI is the 'voice' of British business.

CONSULTANTS REGISTER

79 Mansel Street, Swansea SA1 5TY
T: 01792 551468 F: 01792 465286
E: enquiries@consultantsregister.co.uk
W: www.consultantsregister.co.uk
[Consultants]
An online source of consultants, searchable by category.

CO-OPERATIVE BANK PLC

PO Box 101, 1 Balloon Street, Manchester M60 4EP
T: 01695 53760
E: business.direct@co-operativebank.co.uk
W: www.co-operativebank.co.uk
[Debt]
The Co-operative Bank offers a full range of banking services to small
businesses.

CREATIVE ADVANTAGE FUND

West Midlands Arts, 82 Granville Street, Birmingham B1 2LH
T: 0121 631 3121 F: 0121 643 7239
Fund Manager: Birmingham Venture Capital Ltd, Alpha Tower,
Suffolk Street, Queensway, Birmingham B1 1TR
W: www.creative-advantage-fund.co.uk
[Equity]
A venture capital fund for creative businesses in the West Midlands.

CRESCENT CAPITAL

5 Crescent Gardens, Belfast BT7 1NS
T: 028 9023 3633 F: 028 9032 9525
E: mail@crescentcapital.co.uk W: www.crescentcapital.co.uk
[Equity]
A Belfast-based venture capital fund, specialising in early-stage to
MBO Northern Ireland investments between £250,000 and £750,000.

DELOITTE & TOUCHE

Stonecutter Court, 1 Stonecutter Street, London EC4A 4TR
T: 0207 936 3000 F: 0207 583 1198
W: www.deloitte.com/uk/
[Accountants; Consultants]
Deloitte & Touche is a leading professional services firm, which offers
assurance and advisory, tax, and consulting services.

DEPARTMENT FOR EMPLOYMENT & LEARNING
(Northern Ireland)

Adelaide House, 39-49 Adelaide Street, Belfast BT2 8FD
T: 028 9025 7777 F: 028 9025 7778
E: del@nics.gov.uk W: www.tea-ni.org.uk
[Training]
The Department for Employment & Learning is responsible for third
level education, training and a range of employment measures.

DEPARTMENT FOR ENVIRONMENT, FOOD & RURAL AFFAIRS

Ergon House, 17 Smith Square, London SW1P 3JR
T: 0845 933 5577
W: www.defra.gov.uk
[Community & Rural Development; Policy]
DEFRA is responsible for sustainable development, food and farming,
rural communities.

DEPARTMENT FOR WORK & PENSIONS

The Adelphi, 1-11 John Adam Street, London WC2N 6HT
T: 0207 712 2171 F: 0207 712 2386
W: www.dwp.gov.uk
[Policy]
The Department is responsible for delivering support and advice
through a network of services to people of working age, employers,
pensioners, families and children and disabled people.

DEPARTMENT OF AGRICULTURE & RURAL DEVELOPMENT (Northern Ireland)

Dundonald House, Upper Newtownards Road, Belfast BT4 3SB
T: 028 9052 4999 F: 028 9052 5003
[Community & Rural Development; Policy]
DARDNI is responsible for the agricultural, forestry and fishing
industries, rural development, agricultural research and education
and application of EU agricultural policy in Northern Ireland.

DEPARTMENT OF ENTERPRISE, TRADE & INVESTMENT (Northern Ireland)

Netherleigh, Massey Avenue, Belfast BT4 2JP
T: 028 9052 9900 F: 028 9052 9550
E: information@detini.gov.uk W: www.detini.gov.uk
[Policy]
The Department of Enterprise, Trade & Investment is responsible for
economic development in Northern Ireland.

DEPARTMENT OF TRADE & INDUSTRY

1 Victoria Street, London SW1W 0ET
T: 0207 215 5000
E: eqnquiries@dti.gsi.gov.uk W: www.dti.gov.uk
[Policy]
DTI sets policy, objectives ands strategy for wealth-creation in Britain.

DEVELOPMENT TRUSTS ASSOCIATION

2-8 Scrutton Street, London EC2A 4RT
T: 0845 458 8336 F: 0845 458 8337
E: info@dta.org.uk W: www.dta.org.uk
[Community & Rural Development]
DTA is a community-based regeneration network. Its website lists its
members.

DHP ENTERPRISE

Scientific Centre, 70 Corporation Road, Middlesbrough TS1 2RJ
T: 01642 244359 F: 01642 244316
E: info@dhp-enterprise.co.uk W: www.dhp-enterprise.co.uk
[Start-Up Training]
DHP Enterprise is a business support agency that provides training &
advice. It also operates in Scotland, as DHP Scotland. See also *Bethany
Group*.

DURHAM BUSINESS SCHOOL

University of Durham, Mill Hill Lane, Durham DH1 3LB
T: 0191 334 5200 F: 0191 334 5201
W: www.dur.ac.uk/udbs/
[Training]
Durham Business School (DUBS) helps businesses to help themselves
through consultancy, networking and training activities.

EAST MIDLANDS DEVELOPMENT AGENCY

Apex Court, City Link, Nottingham, NG2 4LA
T: 0115 988 8300 F: 0115 8533666
E: info@emd.org.uk W: www.emda.org.uk
**[Community & Rural Development; Enterprise Support; Grants;
Incubator; Inwards Investment; Policy]**
One of the nine *Regional Development Agencies* established by the
Government in 1999/2000 to promote the sustainable economic
development of the regions. Emda's role is to champion the region's
economy and its development, increase business competitiveness,
attract new business and create jobs and regenerate local
communities. See also *SeekingFinance.co.uk*.

EAST OF ENGLAND DEVELOPMENT AGENCY

The Business Centre, Station Road, Histon, Cambridge CB4 9LQ
T: 01223 713900 F: 01223 713940
E: knowledge@eeda.org.uk W: www.eeda.org.uk
**[Community & Rural Development; Enterprise Support; Grants;
Incubator; Inwards Investment; Policy]**
One of the nine *Regional Development Agencies* established by the
Government in 1999/2000 to promote the sustainable economic
development of the regions. EEDA has a wide-ranging remit that
includes economic development and social and physical
regeneration, as well as business support, investment and
competitiveness. EEDA administers the Regional Selective Assistance
scheme. It plans to develop a network of enterprise Hubs, as well as a
programme supporting new innovation and incubator centres,
innovation and technology parks, with a particular focus on high
added value start-ups, high-growth clusters and key sectors.

EGRINDSTONE.CO.UK

W: www.egrindstone.co.uk
[Information; Website]
This website shares the developers' experiences of working from
home, both positive and negative.

ENTERPRISE NORTHERN IRELAND

Aghanloo Industrial Estate, Aghanloo Road, Limavady BT49 OHE
T: 028 7776 2323
W: www.enterpriseni.com
[Information]
Enterprise Northern Ireland is the association of 32 Enterprise
Agencies in Northern Ireland. It provides support for business start-
ups, micro business, established business, and the social economy.
There are Enterprise Agencies in:

- Antrim
- Ballycastle
- Ballymena
- Ballymoney
- Banbridge
- Bangor
- Belfast (8)
- Carrickfergus
- Coleraine
- Cookstown
- Downpatrick
- Draperstown
- Dungannon
- Enniskillen
- Larne
- Limavaddy

- Lisburn
- Londonderry
- Newry
- Newtownabbey

- Newtownards
- Omagh
- Strabane.

ENTREPRENEURIAL EXCHANGE

Barncluith Business Centre, Townhead Street, Hamilton ML3 7DP
T: 01698 285650 F: 01698 540132
E: info@entrepreneurial-exchange.co.uk
W: www.entrepreneurial-exchange.co.uk
[**Networking**]
The Entrepreneurial Exchange is Scotland's leading members'
organisation for ambitious, growth-orientated entrepreneurs,
providing networking and business opportunities.

ENTREPRENEURS' NETWORK CLUB

Suite 1, Fourways House, 57 Hilton Street, Manchester M1 2EJ
T: 07766 408815
W: www.enc-network.co.uk
[**Networking**]
ENC offers fortnightly meetings where new and start-up businesses
can get together and gain the support to help them through the early
stages of development.

ENVIRONMENT AGENCY

T: 0845 933 3111
E: enquiries@environment-agency.gov.uk
W: www.environment-agency.gov.uk
[**Information; Regulator & Standards**]
The Environment Agency is a non-departmental body that aims to
protect and improve the environment and support sustainable
development.

EQUITYGAP LTD

Hillington Park Innovation Centre, 1 Ainslie Road, Hillington G52 1RU
T: 0141 585 6333 F: 0141 585 6301
E: enquiries@equitygap.com W: www.equitygap.com
[Business Angels; Equity]
Equitygap is the largest active Business Angel syndicate operating in
the West of Scotland. Its website allows entrepreneurs to present their
proposal directly to the syndicate members.

EQUITYNETWORK

InterTradeIreland, The Old Gasworks Business Park,
Kilmorey Street, Newry, Co. Down BT34 2DE
T: 028 3083 4151 F: 028 3083 4155
E: equity@intertradeireland.com W: www.intertradeireland.com
[Business Angels; Equity]
A division of *InterTradeIreland*, EquityNetwork provides free, value-
added advisory services to businesses in Northern Ireland to assist in
making them 'investor-ready', as well as signposting and advice for
businesses seeking equity finance.

ERNST & YOUNG

Rolls House, 7 Rolls Buildings, Fetter Lane, London EC4A 1NH
T: 0207 951 2000 F: 0207 951 4001
W: www.ey.com/uk
[Accountants; Consultants]
Ernst & Young provide audit, accounting, taxation and payroll
services for companies of all sizes.

EUROPA

W: europa.eu.int
[EU Support]
The European Union's website, Europa, features information on the
objectives of the EU, details on its agencies and the latest news. The
URL http://europa.eu.int/comm/enterprise/index_en.htm is specific
to enterprise matters.

EUROPEAN COMMISSION

8 Storey's Gate, London SW1P 3AT
T: 0207 973 1992 F: 0207 973 1900/1910
E: Jim.Dougal@cec.eu.int W: www.europe.org.uk
[EU Support]
To help small and medium-sized businesses (SMEs), the European
Commission has funded various programmes (see **Chapter 9**).

EUROPEAN INFORMATION CENTRES

W: www.euro-info.org.uk
[EU Support; Information]
Euro Info Centres (EICs) provide local access to a range of specialist
information and advisory services to help companies develop their
business in Europe. EICs in Britain include:

- Belfast
- Birmingham
- Bradford
- Bristol
- Chelmsford
- Durham
- Exeter
- Glasgow
- Hull
- Inverness
- Leeds
- Leicester
- Liverpool
- London
- Manchester
- Newcastle
- Norwich
- Nottingham
- Sheffield
- Slough
- Southampton
- St Albans
- Wales
- West Malling, Kent.

EVERYWOMAN.CO.UK

12 Hurlingham Business Park, Sulivan Road, London SW6 3DU
T: 0870 746 1800
E: info@everywoman.co.uk W: www.everywoman.co.uk
[Information; Networking; Website; Women]
Everywoman.co.uk is an independent community site for women in
business, offering information, advice and support to women who are
starting-up or growing their own business.

EW-NETWORK

W: www.ew-network.com
[Information; Networking; Website; Women]
ew-network is a network and community for UK businesswomen.

FASTLINKSOLUTIONS.CO.UK

W: www.fastlinksolutions.co.uk
[Information; Website]
A broad range of free content for business start-ups, including small
business planning, market research, legal aspects, costing/pricing,
sales forecasts, cash flow and profit and loss forecasts, writing a
business plan, and effective sales and promotion.

FEDERATION OF SMALL BUSINESSES

Whittle Way, Blackpool Business Park, Blackpool, Lancs FY4 2FE
T: 01253 336000
W: www.fsb.org.uk
[Networking]
FSB is a membership organisation for small businesses.

FINANCE WALES

Oakleigh House, Park Place, Cardiff CF10 3DQ
T: 029 2033 8100 F: 029 2033 8101
E: info@financewales.co.uk W: www.financewales.co.uk
[Information]
A wholly owned subsidiary of the *Welsh Development Agency*,
Finance Wales helps SMEs in Wales to realise their true potential for
innovation and growth by bridging the 'funding gap', the difficulty,
which many new and small Welsh businesses have experienced in
raising finance.

FIRST TRUST BANK

92 Ann Street, Belfast, BT1 3AY
Tel: 028 9032 5599 F: 028 9032 1754
W: www.firsttrustbank.co.uk
[Debt]
First Trust Bank is *Allied Irish Bank*'s Northern Ireland business
banking service.

FIRST TUESDAY

W: www.firsttuesday.co.uk
[Business Angels; E-Business; Networking]
First Tuesday is a monthly forum (held, as the name suggests, on the
first Tuesday of every month) and open marketplace for
entrepreneurs, start-ups, investors and service providers in the new
economy. Every month, top-tier Internet entrepreneurs address the
community, sharing lessons learned and how they implemented their
personal visions. See also *First Tuesday Scotland*.

FIRST TUESDAY SCOTLAND

The Hexagon Building, Kelvin Campus,
West of Scotland Science Park, Glasgow G20 OSP
T: 0141 946 4433
E: gordon@firsttuesdayscotland.com
W: www.firsttuesdayscotland.com
[Business Angels; E-Business; Networking]
See *First Tuesday*.

FORUM OF PRIVATE BUSINESS

Ruskin Chambers, Drury Lane, Knutsford, Cheshire WA16 6HA
T: 01565 634467 F: 0870 458 2516
E: fpbltd@fpb.co.uk W: www.fpb.co.uk
[Information; Networking]
FPB supports its members with information and advice and by
lobbying to influence legislation that affects small businesses. See
Forum of Private Business in Scotland.

FORUM OF PRIVATE BUSINESS IN SCOTLAND

Unit 4 Alpha Centre, Stirling University Innovation Park,
Stirling FK9 4NF
T/F: 0786 472450
E: gerry.dowds@fpb.co.uk W: www.fpb.co.uk
[Information; Networking]
See *Forum of Private Business*.

FRANCHISEDIRECT.COM

McGarry Consulting, 102 Pembroke Road, Dublin 4, Ireland
T: 00 353 1 668 5444 F: 00 353 1 668 5541
E: smcgarry@franchisedirect.com W: www.franchisedirect.com
[Franchises; Information]
This website provides views, news and advice to entrepreneurs and
franchisers, including a directory of franchisers seeking franchisees.

GET INTO ENTERPRISE

Careers Scotland, 150 Broomielaw, Atlantic Quay, Glasgow G2 8LU
T: 0141 228 2073
E: betty.orr@scotent.co.uk W: www.getintoenterprise.com
[Start-Up Training]
Get into Enterprise Online aims to develop enterprise skills in people
of all ages and backgrounds, through a 12-module programme that
has Scottish Qualifications Authority accreditation. Careers Scotland is
part of *Scottish Enterprise* and *Highlands & Islands Enterprise*.

GETFINANCE.CO.UK

W: www.getfinance.co.uk
[Information; Website]
This website lists venture capital organisations and other sources of
business finance.

GOVERNMENT DIRECT FOR BUSINESS

W: www.nics.gov.uk/ni-direct/
[Information; Website]
This website provides information on government regulations
applicable to Northern Ireland, as well as common business forms.

GOVERNMENT INFORMATION SERVICE

See *UK Online*.

GOVERNMENT OFFICES
[Policy]

Part of the Office of the Deputy Prime Minister, Government Offices
bring together the activities of a number of Government Departments
to ensure a co-ordinated approach within each region, including:

- Department for Culture Media & Sport (DCMS)
- Department for Education and Skills (DfES)
- Department for Transport (DfT)
- Department for Work and Pensions (DWP)
- Department of Environment, Food & Rural Affairs (DEFRA)
- Department of Health (DOH)
- Department of Trade and Industry (DTI)
- Home Office (HO)
- Office of the Deputy Prime Minister (ODPM).

Government Offices also work with local partners and organisations
within the region. They administer national and European grant
programmes, such as the European Social Fund (ESF) and the
European Regional Development Fund (ERDF). There are
Government Offices for:

- East Midlands
- East of England
- London
- North East
- North West
- South East
- South West
- West Midlands
- Yorkshire & the Humber.

GRANTFINDER

Enterprise House, Carlton Road, Worksop, Nottinghamshire S81 7QF
T: 01909 501200
E: enquiries@grantfinder.co.uk W: www.grantfinder.co.uk
[Grants; Information; Website]

A source of information on UK and EU financial support provision,
including grants, subsidies, loans, venture funding and other
incentives, available to all types of business.

GROWING BUSINESS AWARDS

Real Business, 23rd Floor, Millbank Tower, Millbank,
London SW1P 4QP
T: 0207 828 0999 F: 0207 630 0733
E: awards@caspianpublishing.co.uk
W: www.growingbusinessawards.co.uk
[**Competitions**]
The Growing Business Awards are open to all businesses with up to
500 employees. They are backed by the CBI, the leading voice of
British business, and *Real Business*, a magazine for the UK's
entrepreneurs.

HARCOURT BUSINESS SYSTEMS

Metro House, Northgate, Chichester, West Sussex PO19 1BE
T: 07050 125560
E: info@harcourtbusiness.com W: www.harcourtbusiness.com
[**Business Plans**]
Developer and publisher of Step-by-Step business planning software.

HEALTH & SAFETY EXECUTIVE

HSE Infoline, Caerphilly Business Park, Caerphilly CF83 3GG
T: 08701 545500 F: 029 2085 9260
E: hseinformationservices@natbrit.com
[**Information; Regulator & Standards**]
All employers, including the self-employed have duties under the
Health and Safety at Work etc Act 1974, to ensure their workplace is
safe. HSE Infoline is a 'one-stop shop', providing rapid access to HSE's
wealth of health and safety information, and access to expert advice
and guidance.

HEALTH & SAFETY EXECUTIVE FOR NORTHERN IRELAND

83 Ladas Drive, Belfast BT6 9FR
T: 028 9024 3249 F: 028 9023 5383
E: hseni@detini.gov.uk W: www.hseni.gov.uk
[**Information; Publications; Regulator & Standards**]
HSENI has published a *Guide to Workplace Health & Safety*, illustrating
the general scope of the laws covering health and safety at work. The
guide is useful to anyone starting up a new firm, managing a small
work unit, preparing a safety policy for a company or looking for
general health and safety information.

HIGHLANDS & ISLANDS ENTERPRISE

Cowan House, Inverness Retail and Business Park, Inverness IV2 7GF
T: 01463 234171
E: hie.general@hient.co.uk W: www.hie.co.uk
[Information; Website]
See also *Business Information Source in Highland Scotland.*

HM CUSTOMS & EXCISE

T: 0845 010 9000
W: www.hmce.gov.uk
[Information; Regulator & Standards; Website]
For advice on VAT, contact your nearest VAT Business Advice Centre.
HM Customs & Excise's website provides a list of centres. HM
Customs & Excise also holds Business Advice Open Days.

HOME BUSINESS ALLIANCE

FREEPOST ANG3155, March, Cambridgeshire PE15 9BR
T: 0870 749 6321 F: 0870 749 6322
E: info@homebusiness.org.uk W: www.homebusiness.org.uk
[Information; Networking]
A trade association that specialises in home businesses.

HSBC

8 Canada Square, London E14 5HQ
W: www.hsbc.co.uk
[Debt]
Voted 'Best Clearing Bank for Small Business 2002' by the *Forum of
Private Business.*

IBIS ASSOCIATES

14 Scotney Road, Basingstoke, Hants RG21 5SR
T: 01256 429349 F: 01256 429350
E: info@ibisassoc.co.uk W: www.ibisassoc.co.uk
[Business Plans; Training]
Ibis Associates provides Business monitoring and performance
enhancement services to start-ups and existing companies. Its
website offers an 'Entrepreneur's Quiz'. It also provides training in
business planning, using *Palo Alto Software*'s Business Plan
Pro/Premier.

ICASS

36 North Hanover Street, George House, Glasgow G1 2AD
T: 0845 601 1718
[R&D]
Supported by European funding, the Innovator's Counselling and
Advisory Service for Scotland provides specialist advice and
counselling for Scotland's inventors and small innovative companies.
A network of counsellors provide this free and confidential service.

IMPERIAL COLLEGE ENTREPRENEURSHIP CENTRE

8 Prince's Gardens, London SW7 1NA
T: 0207 594 9190 F: 0207 594 9191
E: ec@ic.ac.uk W: www.ec.ms.ic.ac.uk/entrepreneurshipcentre/
[Competitions]
The Entrepreneurship Centre provides students with the opportunity
to explore entrepreneurial ideas and develop practical
entrepreneurial skills. The Imperial College's Entrepreneurs
Challenge, an annual business plan competition for Imperial College
students with total prize money of £55,000, is organised by *Nuventis
Partners*.

INBIZ

Enterprise House, 8 Yarm Road, Stockton on Tees TS18 3NA
T: 01642 610610 F: 01642 610611
E: info@inbiz.co.uk W: www.inbizonline.co.uk
[Start-up Training; Training]
InBiz provides specialist support to the long term unemployed and
benefit dependent individuals wishing to move into self-employment.
The leading UK provider of business start-up support, InBiz has 35
offices throughout the UK (see website for contact details).

INDUSTRIAL COMMON OWNERSHIP MOVEMENT LIMITED

Holyoake House, Hanover Street, Manchester M60 0AS
T: 0161 246 2900 F: 0161 831 7684
E: icom@icom.org.uk
[Co-operatives; Social Economy; Training]
ICOM is a membership organisation which promotes the democratic
control and ownership of enterprises by the people who work in
them. It provides a legal advice and registration service, and training
programmes.

INLAND REVENUE

T: 0845 915 4515

W: www.inlandrevenue.gov.uk

[Information; Regulator & Standards; Website]

The Inland Revenue provides an effective and fair tax service to the
country and Government. A guide on the taxation and other
implications of starting a business is available on its website at
www.inlandrevenue.gov.uk/startingup. The website also provides
a list of Inland Revenue offices throughout Britain

INNOVATEUR

E: hc@innovateur.co.uk

W: www.innovation-dynamics.co.uk

[Information; Website]

Innovateur enables entrepreneurs with high-growth-potential projects
to access and leverage resources to achieve their visions. It is a free
resource established and funded by entrepreneurs, for
entrepreneurs.

INNOVATION RELAY CENTRES

W: www.cordis.lu/irc/

[R&D]

A European Commission-funded network of over 60 centres across
Europe that assist companies, universities, research institutes and the
public sector with the process of technology transfer, promote the
exploitation of research results and to provide assistance in applying
for EU research and technological development funding. There are
eight IRCs in the UK including:

- IRC East of England
- IRC Midlands
- IRC North of England
- IRC Northern Ireland
- IRC Scotland
- IRC South East England
- IRC South West England
- IRC Wales.

INSTITUTE FOR SMALL BUSINESS AFFAIRS

1st Floor, 397 Harrogate Road, Leeds LS17 6DJ
T: 0113 393 0241 F: 0113 393 0132
E: info@isbauk.org W: www.isbauk.org
[Information; Networking; Policy]
A membership organisation that encourages high quality research in
the field of small business development and disseminates the findings
for discussion, to assist and inform those responsible for the
formulation, development, implementation and evaluation of
enterprise policy.

INSTITUTE OF ASIAN BUSINESSES

c/o Birmingham Chamber of Commerce and Industry,
Chamber House, 75 Harborne Road, Birmingham B15 3DH
T: 0121 607 8090 F: 0121 607 9899
E: iab@birminghamchamber.org.uk
W: www.iab-birmingham.org.uk
[Minorities & Disabilities]
The Institute of Asian Businesses (IAB) promotes awareness of, and
facilitates solutions to, the business needs of its members and the
wider Asian business community.

INSTITUTE OF BUSINESS ADVISERS

Response House, Queen Street North, Chesterfield S41 9AB UK
T: 01246 453322 F: 01246 453300
E: enquiries@iba.org.uk W: www.iba.org.uk
[Consultants; Mentoring; Training]
IBA's membership comprises business advisers, counsellors, mentors
and trainers who specialise in helping small firms. Check the IBA
website for details of your nearest branch.

INSTITUTE OF CHARTERED ACCOUNTANTS
IN ENGLAND & WALES

Moorgate Place, London EC2P 2BJ
T: 0207 920 8100
W: www.icaew.co.uk
[Accountants]
ICAEW is one of the accountancy bodies whose members are
permitted to audit company accounts. If you're looking for an
accountant, ICAEW can direct you to one of its members.

INSTITUTE OF CHARTERED ACCOUNTANTS IN IRELAND

Northern Ireland office, 11 Donegall Square South, Belfast BT1 5JE
T: 028 9032 1600 F: 028 9023 0071
E: ca@icai.ie W: www.icai.ie
[Accountants]
ICAI is one of the accountancy bodies whose members are permitted
to audit company accounts. If you're looking for an accountant, ICAI
can direct you to one of its members.

INSTITUTE OF CHARTERED ACCOUNTANTS IN SCOTLAND

CA House, 21 Haymarket Yards, Edinburgh EH12 5BH
T: 0131 347 0100
E: enquiries@icas.org.uk W: www.icas.org.uk
[Accountants]
ICAS is one of the accountancy bodies whose members are permitted
to audit company accounts. If you're looking for an accountant, ICAS
can direct you to one of its members.

INSTITUTE OF DIRECTORS

116 Pall Mall, London SW1Y 5ED
T: 0207 839 1233 F: 0207 930 1949
W: www.iod.com
[Information; Networking; Training]
The IoD is a non-political business organisation founded by Royal
Charter in 1903, dedicated to providing directors with the information
and advice they require to help their business succeed.

INSTITUTE OF LEADERSHIP & MANAGEMENT

1 Giltspur Street, London EC1A 9DD
T: 0207 294 2470 F: 0207 294 2402
E: marketing@i-l-m.com W: www.i-l-m.com
[Training]
ILM offers Business Start-Up and Development Qualifications
designed to ensure the success of new business start-ups and the
development of existing small- and medium-sized enterprises (SMEs).

INTELLECTUAL PROPERTY UK

W: www.intellectual-property.gov.uk
[Intellectual Property]
A Government-backed website, with information on all aspects of intellectual property (copyright, designs, patents and trademarks).

INTERTRADEIRELAND

The Old Gasworks Business Park, Kilmorey Street, Newry,
Co. Down BT34 2DE
T: 028 3083 4151 F: 028 3083 4155
E: info@intertradeireland.com W: www.intertradeireland.com
[Enterprise Support; Information; Policy]
InterTradeIreland's remit is to accelerate trade and business development across the whole island of Ireland. See also *EquityNetwork*.

INVESTNI

64 Chichester Street, Belfast BT1 4JX
T: 028 9023 9090 F: 028 9049 0490
E: info@investni.com W: www.investni.com
[Enterprise Support; Information; Inwards Investment]
For assistance and information on business start-up in Northern Ireland. InvestNI has Regional Information Centres in:

- Ballymena
- Londonderry
- Newry
- Omagh.

INVESTORS IN PEOPLE

7-10 Chandos Street, London W1G 9DQ
T: 0207 467 1900 F: 0207 636 2386
E: information@iipuk.co.uk W: www.investorsinpeople.co.uk
[Regulator & Standards]
Investors in People UK is responsible for the promotion, quality assurance and development of the Investors in People National Standard.

ISIS INNOVATION LTD

Ewert House, Ewert Place, Summertown, Oxford OX2 7SG
T: 01865 280830 F: 01865 280831
E: innovation@isis.ox.ac.uk W: www.isis-innovation.com
[R&D]
Isis Innovation is a wholly owned subsidiary of the University of
Oxford, founded to exploit know-how arising out of research at its
research institutions. Isis provides researchers with commercial
advice, funds patent applications and legal costs, and negotiates
exploitation and spin-out company agreements, and identifies and
manages consultancy opportunities for University researchers.

J4B.CO.UK

51 Water Lane, Wilmslow, Cheshire SK9 5BQ
E: enquiries@j4b.co.uk W: www.j4b.co.uk
[Grants; Information; Website]
A free searchable database of grants and funding opportunities.

JOBCENTRE PLUS

Level 6, Caxton House, Tothill Street, London SW1H 9NA
W: www.jobcentreplus.gov.uk
[Start-Up Training]
Unemployed people thinking of starting a business can access a
range of training/benefit schemes. Ask about Business Start-up at
your local JobCentre, *Business Links* (in England), the *Small Business
Gateway* (in Scotland) or *Business Connect* (in Wales).

KPMG

8 Salisbury Square, London EC4Y 8BB
T: 0207 311 1000 F: 0207 311 3311
W: www.kmpg.co.uk
[Accountants; Consultants]
KPMG is a major firm of chartered accountants and business advisers,
providing services to clients in all sectors business. It is the UK
national practice of KPMG International.

LAW SOCIETY

113 Chancery Lane, London WC2A 1PL
T: 0207 242 1222
E: info.services@lawsoc.org.uk W: www.lawsoc.org.uk
[Legal]
The Law Society is an educational, representative and regulatory
body and exercises statutory functions in relation to the education,
admission, enrolment, discipline and regulation of the solicitors'
profession. If you're looking for a lawyer, the Law Society can direct
you to one of its members.

LAW SOCIETY OF NORTHERN IRELAND

Law Society House, 98 Victoria Street, Belfast BT1 3JZ
T: 028 9023 1614 F: 028 9023 2606
E: info@lawsoc-ni.org W: www.lawsoc-ni.org
[Legal]
The Law Society regulates the solicitors' profession in Northern
Ireland with the aim of protecting the public. If you're looking for a
lawyer, it can direct you to one of its members (see *Lawyers for Your
Business*).

LAW SOCIETY OF SCOTLAND

26 Drumsheugh Gardens, Edinburgh EH3 7YR
T: 0131 226 7411 F: 0131 225 2934
E: lawscot@lawscot.org.uk W: www.lawscot.org.uk
[Legal]
The Law Society of Scotland is an educational, representative and
regulatory body and exercises statutory functions in relation to the
education, admission, enrolment, discipline and regulation of the
solicitors' profession in Scotland. If you're looking for a lawyer, the
Law Society can direct you to one of its members.

LAWYERS FOR YOUR BUSINESS

T: 0207 405 9075
[Legal]
Operated by the Law Society, this scheme helps you find a solicitor –
just telephone the helpline number.

LEARN DIRECT FOR BUSINESS

W: www.learndirect-business.co.uk
[**Training**]
A source of online training aimed at businesses.

LEARNING & SKILLS COUNCIL

Cheylesmore House, Quinton Road, Coventry CV1 2WT
T: 0845 019 4170 F: 024 7649 3600
E: info@lsc.gov.uk W: www.lsc.gov.uk
[**Training**]
The Learning and Skills Council is responsible for funding and
planning education and training for over 16-year-olds in England. Its
aim is to raise participation and attainment through high-quality
education and training, putting learners first. There are 47 local
Learning and Skills Councils across England.

LINC SCOTLAND

Queens House, 19 St Vincent Place, Glasgow G1 2DT
T: 0141 221 3321
W: www.lincscot.co.uk
[**Business Angels; Equity**]
The Local Investment Networking Company is an independent not-
for-profit organisation acting as the national business angel network
for Scotland. It offers a nationwide business introduction network or
'marriage bureau' for companies and investors.

LLOYDS TSB BANK PLC

25 Gresham Street, London EC2V 7HN
T: 0845 072 5555
W: www.lloydstsb.com
[**Debt**]
Lloyds TSB offers start-up customers three years of discounted
banking, credit interest, and a range of solutions tailored to start-up
businesses, including *Success4Business.com*. See also
SmallBusiness.co.uk.

LLOYDS TSB SCOTLAND PLC

Henry Duncan House, 120 George Street, Edinburgh EH2 4LH
T: 0845 072 5555
W: www.lloydstsb.com
[Debt]
Lloyds TSB Scotland offers start-up customers in Scotland three years
of discounted banking, credit interest, and a range of solutions
tailored to start-up businesses, including *Success4Business.com*. See
also *SmallBusiness.co.uk*.

LOCAL ENTERPRISE AGENCIES

See **www.nfea.com** for a full list of LEAs.
[Enterprise Support; Information]
Local Enterprise Agencies (LEAs) are typically partnerships between
the private sector and local authorities, with support from central
Government. They deliver business support services (training,
information, advice and counselling) under contract, to the *Learning
and Skills Council*, to *Business Links*, and to the Single Regeneration
Budget (SRB), drawing on a local network of specialist skills, such as
accountants, lawyers and banks. See also *National Federation of
Enterprise Agencies* and *SmallBusinessAdvice.org.uk*.

LONDON DEVELOPMENT AGENCY

Devon House, 58-60 St Katherine's Way, London E1W 1JX
T: 0207 680 2000 F: 0207 680 2014/2040
W: www.lda.gov.uk
**[Community & Rural Development; Enterprise Support; Grants;
Incubator; Inwards Investment; Policy; Social Economy]**
One of the nine *Regional Development Agencies* established by the
Government in 1999/2000 to promote the sustainable economic
development of the regions. It reports to an elected Mayor of London.
It operates *London Innovation,* the *Capital Fund,* Up & Running
(support for early start-ups through *Business Link London*) and
Enterprise for Communities, supporting the social economy.

London Innovation

Innovation Unit, London Development Agency, Devon House,
58 - 60 St Katherines Way, London E1W 1JX
E: innovation@lda.gov.uk W: www.london-innovation.org.uk
[R&D]
A division of the *London Development Agency*, London Innovation
ensures that innovation is encouraged, supported and exploited
throughout the region.

Mentor Wales

Finance Wales PLC, QED Centre, Main Avenue,
Treforest Industrial Estate, Treforest CF37 5YR
T: 01443 845891 F: 01443 845828
W: www.mentorwales.co.uk
[Mentoring]
Mentor Wales provides long-term support from very experienced
business people who are available to work with participating
companies up to a two-year period.

Mercia Enterprise Fund

West Midlands Enterprise Ltd, Wellington House,
31-34 Waterloo Street, Birmingham B2 5TJ
W: www.merciafund.co.uk
[Equity]
A seed capital fund to support the commercialisation of technology
through new start-up companies in the West Midlands.

Minority Business Form

W: www.minorities4business.co.uk
[Minorities & Disabilities]
The Forum is an independent advisory body representing the
interests of minority ethnic businesses across the West Midlands.

MINTEL INTERNATIONAL GROUP LTD

18-19 Long Lane, London EC1A 9PL
T: 0207 606 4533 F: 0207 606 5932
E: info@mintel.com W: www.mintel.com
[Information; Marketing]
A supplier of competitive media, product and consumer intelligence
on all aspects of consumers' economic activity.

MYFRANCHISE.NET

The Franchise Alliance, St Paul's Gate, Cross Street
Winchester SO23 8SZ
T: 01962 849 456 T: 01962 849 555
E: info@myfranchise.net W: www.myfranchise.net
[Franchises; Information]
Free franchise seminars, with online booking. Supported by *NatWest*.

NATIONAL ASSEMBLY OF WALES

Cardiff Bay, Cardiff CF99 1NA
T: 029 2082 5111
W: www.wales.gov.uk
[Policy]

NATIONAL BUSINESS ANGELS NETWORK

40-42 Cannon Street, London EC4N 6JJ
T: 0207 329 2929 F: 0207 329 2626
W: www.nationalbusangels.co.uk
[Business Angels; Equity]
A membership network for business angels.

NATIONAL ENDOWMENT FOR SCIENCE, TECHNOLOGY & THE ARTS

Fishmongers' Chambers, 110 Upper Thames Street,
London EC4R 3TW
T: 0207 645 9500
E: nesta@nesta.org.uk W: www.nesta.org.uk
[R&D]
NESTA provides a step-by-step guide to the process of invention and
innovation. It invests in ideas it thinks will give a return: commercial,
social, cultural or all three.

NATIONAL EXTENSION COLLEGE

Michael Young Centre, Purbeck Road, Cambridge CB2 2HN
T: 01223 400 350 F: 01223 400 325
E: info@nec.ac.uk W: www.nec.ac.uk
[Start-Up Training; Training]
The National Extension College is a non-profit making trust
dedicated to widening access to education for adults through distance
learning. It offers a Business Start-up course, covering the knowledge
and skills needed to start up your own business, from financial and
legal planning to market testing, business planning, securing
premises, customers and suppliers. The course also provides the
underpinning knowledge for an Owner Management S/NVQ.

NATIONAL FEDERATION OF ENTERPRISE AGENCIES

Trinity Gardens, 9-11 Bromham Road, Bedford MK40 2UQ
T: 01234 354055
E: enquiries@nfea.com W: www.nfea.com
[Enterprise Support; Mentoring]
NFEA is a network of independent, but not-for-profit, *Local Enterprise
Agencies* providing a range of services targeted at pre-start, start-up
and micro businesses, to help build their ability to survive, to sustain
themselves and to grow. It manages the *British Volunteer Mentoring
Association*. See also *SmallBusinessAdvice.org.uk*.

NATWEST

135 Bishopsgate, London EC2M 3UR
W: www.natwest.com
[Debt]
The website provides useful basic guidance for start-ups.

NEW BUSINESS - NEW LIFE

T: 0870 774 4000
W: www.newbusiness-newlife.org.uk
[Information; Website]
The New Business - New Life campaign aims to raise awareness on the
potential benefits of starting a business, as well as directing you to
sources of further information and support.

North West Regional Development Agency

PO Box 37, Renaissance House, Centre Park, Warrington,
Cheshire WA1 1XB
T: 01925 400100 F: 01925 400400
E: information@nwda.co.uk W: www.nwda.co.uk
**[Community & Rural Development; Enterprise Support; Grants;
Incubator; Inwards Investment; Policy]**
One of the nine *Regional Development Agencies* established by the
Government in 1999/2000 to promote the sustainable economic
development of the regions. It is responsible for the sustainable
economic development and regeneration of England's Northwest
through the promotion of business competitiveness, efficiency,
investment, employment and skills development.

Northern Bank Ltd

Donegall Square West, Belfast BT1 6JS
T: 028 9024 5277 F: 028 9023 1349
E: geoff.greer@eu.nabgroup.com W: www.nbonline.co.uk
[Debt]
As well as traditional banking services, Northern Bank offers
specialist services in foreign exchange, leasing and hire purchase,
debtor finance, corporate banking and agriculture. Northern Bank is a
member of the National Australia Bank Group, which includes
Clydesdale Bank, *National Irish Bank Limited* and *Yorkshire Bank PLC*.

Northern Ireland Executive

W: www.nics.gov.uk
[Policy]
The Secretary of State for Northern Ireland suspended the Northern
Ireland Assembly and the Executive with effect from midnight on 14
October 2002. The Secretary of State, assisted by his team of Northern
Ireland Office Ministers, has assumed responsibility for the direction
and control of the Northern Ireland Departments. Updates on this
situation will be available on this website.

NORTHERN IRELAND OFFICE

W: www.nio.gov.uk
[Policy]
The Northern Ireland Executive was responsible for policy relating to
agriculture and rural development; culture, arts and leisure;
education; enterprise, trade and investment; environment; finance
and personnel; health, social services and public safety; higher and
further education, training and employment; regional development
and social development. The Secretary of State for Northern Ireland
and the Northern Ireland Office currently hold this responsibility (see
Northern Ireland Executive).

NORTHERN IRELAND STATISTICS AND RESEARCH AGENCY

McAuley House, 2-14 Castle Street, Belfast BT1 1SA
T: 028 9034 8100 F: 028 9034 8106
W: www.nisra.gov.uk
[Information]
NISRA provides statistics, social research and registration services,
and is responsible for the census of population in Northern Ireland.

NUVENTIS PARTNERS

8 Prince's Gardens, South Kensington, London SW7 1NA
W: www.nuventis.co.uk
[Consultants]
Nuventis provides market-led strategic consulting services for
potential high-growth businesses. It also organises the *Imperial
College* Entrepreneur's Challenge.

OAK TREE PRESS

19 Rutland Street, Cork, Ireland
T: 00 353 21 431 3855 F: 00 353 21 431 3496
E: info@oaktreepress.com
W: www.oaktreepress.com / www.startingabusinessinbritain.com
[Publications; Start-Up Training; Training; Website]
An international developer of enterprise training and support
materials, Oak Tree Press' managing director Brian O'Kane is author
of this book and webmaster for the companion website,
www.startingabusinessinbritain.com. Oak Tree Press also
provides training for entrepreneurs and those who support them.

ONENORTHEAST
(REGIONAL DEVELOPMENT AGENCY FOR THE NORTH EAST)

Stella House, Goldcrest Way, Newburn Riverside,
Newcastle upon Tyne NE15 8NY
T: 0191 229 6200 F: 0191 229 6201
W: www.onenortheast.co.uk
[**Community & Rural Development; Enterprise Support; Grants;
Incubator; Inwards Investment; Policy**]
One of the nine *Regional Development Agencies* established by the
Government in 1999/2000 to promote the sustainable economic
development of the regions. Its activities include inwards investment,
site and property development, urban and rural development,
business growth, cluster development, innovation, e-business and ICT
initiatives, employment, skills and education development,
sustainable development, social inclusion and community
development.

OPPORTUNITY WALES.CO.UK

T: 0845 8500 888
W: www.opportunitywales.co.uk
[**E-Business; Information**]
Opportunity Wales helps Small and SMEs throughout Objective One
areas of Wales to take best advantage of the Internet and electronic
commerce.

OXFORD SCIENCE ENTERPRISE CENTRE

Saïd Business School, Park End Street, Oxford OX1 1HP
T: 01865 288800 F: 01865 288805
E: liz.miller@sbs.ox.ac.uk
W: www.science-enterprise.ox.ac.uk/html/Default.asp
[**Competitions**]
Oxford Science Enterprise Centre, part of Oxford University,
encourages entrepreneurship amongst the science and technology
communities in Oxford. It offers an Enterprise Programme, open to all
University members, as well as a business plan competition.

PALO ALTO SOFTWARE

Ivy House, Bradgate Road, London SE6 4JD
T: 0207 610 9371 F: 0207 900 2773
E: info@paloalto.co.uk W: www.paloalto.co.uk
[Business Plans]
Palo Alto Software Limited is the developer of the UK editions of
Business Plan Pro and Business Plan Premier, the award winning
business planning software developed by Palo Alto Software, Inc.
Business Plan Pro/Premier are endorsed by *SFEDI*. It also offers
Business Planning Seminars in association with *Ibis Associates*. See
also *Bplans.org.uk*.

PATENT OFFICE

Concept House, Cardiff Road, Newport NP9 1RH
T: 01633 814000 F: 01633 814444
T: 0845 950 0505 - Advice Line
W: www.patent.gov.uk
[Information; Intellectual Property; Regulator & Standards; R&D]
The Patent Office is responsible for the registration of intellectual
property in the UK.

PHOENIX FUND

[Equity]
The Phoenix Fund is a national fund, designed to encourage
entrepreneurship in disadvantaged areas. Details from *Business Links,
Highlands & Islands Enterprise, Regional Development Agencies* or
Scottish Enterprise.

PLATO ENGLAND

Business Link Wessex, Merck House, Seldown Lane, Poole BH15 1TD
T: 0845 458 8558
E: info@businesslinkwessex.co.uk
W: www.businesslinkwessex.co.uk
[Networking; Training]
PLATO is a business and management development network for
owner/managers of SMEs that starts in 2003. See also *PLATO Ireland*.

PLATO IRELAND

Newry & Mourne Enterprise Agency, Enterprise House,
Canal Quay, Newry, Co Down BT35 6PH
T: 028 3025 1343
W: www.plato.ie
[Networking; Training]
PLATO Ireland is a business and management development network
for owner/managers of SMEs. There are PLATO regional groups in
Belfast and Newry & Mourne. See also *PLATO UK*.

POTENTIA CYMRU

W: www.potentiacymru.co.uk
[Minorities & Disabilities]
Managed by the *Welsh Development Agency*, Potentia provides
support to certain groups facing more barriers than most when setting
up in business such as disabled people, ethnic minorities and young
people.

PRICEWATERHOUSECOOPERS

Southwark Towers, 32 London Bridge Street, London SE1 9SY
T: 0207 583 5000 F: 0207 822 4652
W: www.pwc.com/uk
[Accountants; Consultants]
A major international firm of accountants.

PRINCE'S SCOTTISH YOUTH BUSINESS TRUST

1st Floor, The Guildhall, 57 Queen Street, Glasgow G1 3EN
T: 0141 204 4409 F: 0141 221 8221
E: info@princes-trust.org.uk W: www.princes-trust.org.uk/Scotland/
[Debt; Grants; Start-Up Training; Young Enterprise]
See also *Prince's Trust*, *Prince's Trust Cymru* and *Prince's Trust
Northern Ireland*.

PRINCE'S TRUST

18 Park Square East, London NW1 4LH
T: 0800 842 842 F: 0207 543 1200
E: info@princes-trust.org.uk W: www.princes-trust.org.uk
[Debt; Grants; Start-Up Training; Young Enterprise]
The Prince's Trust provides low interest loans, grants, mentors and
other support for 18-30 year olds who want to start a business.
See also *Prince's Scottish Youth Business Trust*, *Prince's Trust Cymru*
and *Prince's Trust Northern Ireland*.

PRINCE'S TRUST CYMRU

Baltic House, Mount Stuart Square, Cardiff CF10 5FH
T: 029 2043 7000 F: 029 2043 7001
E: info@princes-trust.org.uk W: www.princes-trust.org.uk/Wales/
[Debt; Grants; Start-Up Training; Young Enterprise]
See also *Prince's Scottish Youth Business Trust*, *Prince's Trust* and
Prince's Trust Northern Ireland.

PRINCE'S TRUST NORTHERN IRELAND

Block 5, Jennymount Court, North Derby Street, Belfast BT15 3HN
T: 028 9074 5454 F: 028 9074 8416
E: ptnire@princes-trust.org.uk
W: www.princes-trust.org.uk/Northern Ireland/
[Debt; Grants; Start-Up Training; Young Enterprise]
See also *Prince's Scottish Youth Business Trust*, *Prince's Trust* and
Prince's Trust Cymru.

PROJECT NORTHEAST

Hawthorn House, Forth Banks, Newcastle upon Tyne NE1 3SG
T: 0191 261 7856 F: 0191 261 1910
W: www.pne.org
[Consultants; Equity; Incubator; Training; Youth Enterprise]
PNE companies provide advice, consultancy, finance, training, and
incubator workspace to new and established entrepreneurs in the
region. PNE also runs the *Shell LiveWIRE* programme for the UK.

QUBIS LTD

10 Malone Road, Belfast BT9 5BN
T: 028 9068 2321 F: 028 9066 3015
E: info@qubis.co.uk W: www.qubis.co.uk
[Equity]
Qubis provides equity investment for technology-based businesses
originating from the Queen's University of Belfast.

REGIONAL DEVELOPMENT AGENCIES

Nine agencies were established by the Government in 1999/2000 to
promote the sustainable economic development of the regions. For
contact details and information on the activities of each RDA, see
separate listings. The RDAs cover:

- East Midlands: *East Midlands Development Agency*
- East of England: *East of England Development Agency*
- London: *London Development Agency*
- North East: *OneNorthEast*
- North West: *North West Regional Development Agency*
- South East of England: *South East of England Development Agency*
- South West: *South West Regional Development Agency*
- West Midlands: *Advantage West Midlands*
- Yorkshire and the Humber region: *Yorkshire Forward.*

REGIONAL SELECTIVE ASSISTANCE

See *Regional Development Agencies.*
[Grants]
Regional Selective Assistance (RSA) is a national grant scheme that
provides discretionary grants for projects with fixed capital
expenditure over £500,000 and which create or safeguard jobs. See
also *Regional Selective Assistance Scotland* and *Regional Selective
Assistance Wales.*

REGIONAL SELECTIVE ASSISTANCE SCOTLAND

RSA Scotland - Advice & Appraisal Team, Scottish Executive
Enterprise & Lifelong Learning Department, 5th Floor,
Meridian Court, 5 Cadogan Street, Glasgow G2 6AT
W: www.rsascotland.gov.uk
[Grants]
Regional Selective Assistance (RSA) is a national grant scheme, aimed
at encouraging investment and job creation in the areas of Scotland
designated for regional aid under European Community (EC) law (the
Assisted Areas). Businesses of all sizes can apply for RSA, whether
they are Scottish-owned or owned or headquartered outside Scotland.
It is administered by RSA Scotland, part of the *Scottish Executive*.

REGIONAL SELECTIVE ASSISTANCE WALES

W: www.wales.gov.uk
[Grants]
Regional Selective Assistance supports investment in fixed capital
assets that either preserve or create jobs in assisted areas of Wales.
Fixed capital can include land, buildings, machinery, office and IT
equipment, and other essential costs such as training. The RSA
package is available to new or existing businesses of all sizes in most
business sectors.

REGIONAL VENTURE FUNDS

See *Regional Development Agencies*.
[Equity]
Regional venture Funds have been established in each of the areas
covered by the RDAs. They provide equity investment for high-
growth firms.

ROYAL BANK OF SCOTLAND PLC

36 St Andrew Square, Edinburgh EH2 2YB
T: 0800 521 607
W: www.royalbankscot.co.uk
[Debt]
RBS offers a full range of banking services to small businesses. Its
website offers a financial healthcheck and 'small business clinic'. RBS
owns *NatWest* and *Ulster Bank*.

ROYAL BRITISH LEGION SMALL BUSINESS ADVISORY & LOAN SCHEME

Legion Resettlement Advice, The Cottage, Ordnance Road,
Tidworth, Hants SP9 7QD
T: 01980 843046 F: 01980 847734
E: scracknell@britishlegion.org.uk
[Debt; Information]
The Small Business Advisory and Loan Scheme helps ex-service
personnel planning to start their own business. Loans may also be
available.

RURAL COMMUNITY ENTERPRISE

Business in the Community, 137 Shepherdess Walk, London N1 7RQ
T: 0870 602482 F: 0207 253 1877
W: www.bitc-ruralsignpost.org.uk
**[Community & Rural Development; Information;
Social Economy]**
A source of information on setting up a service, business or
community project in a rural area.

SCHOOL FOR SOCIAL ENTREPRENEURS

18 Victoria Park Square, Bethnal Green, London E29 8F
T: 0208 981 0300 F: 0208 983 4655
W: www.sse.org.uk
[Social Economy; Training]
Training and best practice for social entrepreneurs.

SCOTTISH CHAMBERS OF COMMERCE

30 George Square, Glasgow G2 1EQ
T: 0141 204 8316 F: 0141 221 2336
E: admin@scottishchambers.org.uk
W: www.scottishchambers.org.uk
[Information; Networking; Training]
The Scottish Chambers of Commerce is the umbrella organisation of
all the local Chambers of Commerce in Scotland, including:

- Aberdeen
- Arbroath
- Cumbernauld
- Dalkeith
- Drumnadrochit, Loch Ness

- Dumbarton
- Dumfries
- Dundee
- East Kilbride
- Edinburgh (2)

- Elgin, Morayshire
- Fort William
- Glasgow (2)
- Greenock
- Hamilton
- Helensburgh
- Inverness
- Isle of Mull
- Kilmarnock
- Kingussie
- Kirkcaldy
- Kirkintilloch
- Lanark

- Livingston
- Lochgilphead, Argyll
- Milngavie
- Montrose
- Motherwell
- Oban
- Orkney
- Paisley
- Perth
- Prestwick
- Stornoway, Isle of Lewis
- Stranraer
- Thurso.

SCOTTISH DEVELOPMENT INTERNATIONAL

W: www.scottishdevelopmentinternational.com
[Enterprise Support; Inwards Investment]
Scottish Development International attracts overseas investors into Scotland, and encourages and supports Scottish companies to expand overseas. It is a joint venture between the *Scottish Executive* and *Scottish Enterprise*.

SCOTTISH ENTERPRISE

150 Broomielaw, 5 Atlantic Quay, Glasgow G2 8LU
T: 0141 248 2700 F: 0141 221 3217
[Enterprise Support; Information; Website]
Scottish Enterprise operates offices across Scotland, including:

- Morray Badenoch & Strathspey Enterprise
- Scottish Enterprise Ayrshire
- Scottish Enterprise Borders
- Scottish Enterprise Dumfries & Galloway
- Scottish Enterprise Dunbartonshire
- Scottish Enterprise Edinburgh & Lothian
- Scottish Enterprise Fife
- Scottish Enterprise Forth Valley
- Scottish Enterprise Glasgow
- Scottish Enterprise Grampian
- Scottish Enterprise Lanarkshire

- Scottish Enterprise Renfrewshire
- Scottish Enterprise Tayside
  See also *Small Business Gateway for Lowland Scotland*.

SCOTTISH ENTERPRISE NETWORK

W: www.Scotland.gov.uk/who/elld/enterprise.asp
[Enterprise Suport; Information]
The *Scottish Executive*'s economic development and skills objectives
are promoted in collaboration with *Scottish Enterprise* and *Highlands &
Islands Enterprise* through a network of Local Enterprise Companies
(LECs) that provide support to business start ups, venture capital, and
a range of business services. LECs include:

- Argyll & the Islands
- Ayrshire
- Borders
- Caithness & Sutherland
- Dumfries & Galloway
- Dunbartonshire
- Edinburgh & Lothian
- Fife
- Forth Valley
- Glasgow
- Grampian
- Inverness and Nairn
- Lanarkshire
- Lochaber
- Moray, Badenoch & Strathspey
- Orkney
- Renfrewshire
- Ross and Cromarty
- Shetland
- Skye and Lochalsh
- Tayside
- Western Isles.

SCOTTISH ENVIRONMENT PROTECTION AGENCY

Erskine Court, Castle Business Park, Stirling FK9 4TR
T: 01786 457700 F: 01786 446885
W: www.sepa.org.uk
[Information; Regulator & Standards]
SEPA is responsible for the protection of the environment in Scotland.

SCOTTISH EQUITY PARTNERS LTD

17 Blythswood Square, Glasgow G2 4AD
T: 0141 273 4000 F: 0141 273 4001
E: enquiries@sep.co.uk W: www.scottishdevelopmentfinance.co.uk
[Equity]
Scottish Equity Partners is a privately-owned venture capital firm with
more than 60 years' experience in venture capital investing. Its focus
is on high growth potential technology businesses, typically investing
between £500,000 and £5m in equity financings of up to £20m.

SCOTTISH EXECUTIVE

W: www.scotland.gov.uk
[Policy]
The Scottish Executive is the devolved government for Scotland.
It is responsible for most of the issues of day-to-day concern to the
people of Scotland, including health, education, justice, rural affairs,
and transport.

SCOTTISH INSTITUTE FOR ENTERPRISE

Heriot-Watt University, Edinburgh EH14 4AS
T: 0131 451 8217 F: 0131 451 3193
E: C.J.Queenan@hw.ac.uk W: www.hw.ac.uk/sie/
[R&D]
The Scottish Institute for Enterprise is a cross-university project,
involving all 13 Scottish Universities. Its aim is to increase student
start-ups, especially in science, engineering and technology. SIE
services are open to all students and staff across the Universities.

SCOTTISHBUSINESSWOMEN.COM

W: www.scottishbusinesswomen.com
[Information; Website; Women]
This website provides information on major issues faced by
businesswomen, focussing on how female entrepreneurs tend to
approach business issues. Each page includes pointers to further
sources of help. It is part of an initiative by the *Scottish Enterprise
Network*, *Wellpark Enterprise Centre* and others, in encouraging more
women to unlock their potential.

SEED

PO Box 21293, London W9 1YF
T: 0207 286 3988
E: info@seednetwork.com W: www.seedfusion.com
[Training; Women]
SEED stands for Sustainable Enterprise and Empowerment Dynamics,
the feminine way to do business. SEED provides the support and tools
necessary to starting a business that will create economic
independence as well as make a positive difference to society.

SEEKINGFINANCE.CO.UK

W: www.seekingfinance.co.uk
[Information; Website]
The Seeking Finance website, an initiative of the *East Midlands
Development Agency,* helps businesses in the region to understand
forms of finance appropriate to their business.

SEO-ONLINE.ORG.UK

Community Action Network, The Mezzanine, Elizabeth House,
39 York Road, London SE1 7NQ
T: 0207 401 5321 F: 0207 401 5311
E: contactus@seo-online.org.uk W: www.seo-online.org.uk
[Social Economy]
The seo-online directory is an initiative of *Community Action Network*
and provides advice and information for Social Entrepreneurial
Organisations.

SFEDI - SMALL FIRMS ENTERPRISE DEVELOPMENT INITIATIVE

T: 0114 209 6269
W: www.sfedi.co.uk
[Information; Regulator & Standards]
SFEDI Ltd is government-appointed to identify standards of best
practice for small businesses and those who support them.
It works with practitioners in small business training, education and
advice to make sure that there are good quality, accessible websites,
training products, programmes and qualifications in the market to
help entrepreneurs and endorses suitable products with its logo.
Starting Your Own Business: A Workbook, co-authored by Brian
O'Kane has been endorsed by SFEDI, as has *Palo Alto Software*'s
Business Plan Pro business planning software.

SHELL LIVEWIRE
T: 0845 757 3252
W: www.shell-livewire.org
[Competitions; Young Enterprise]
Shell LiveWIRE helps 16-30 year-olds to start and develop their own
business and hosts an annual competition for business start-ups. The
UK programme is managed by *Project NorthEast*.

SMALL BUSINESS GATEWAY FOR LOWLANDS SCOTLAND
T: 0845 609 6611
E: network.helpline@scotent.co.uk W: www.sbgateway.com
[Information; Website]
The Small Business Gateway is a service provided by the *Scottish
Enterprise Network* and local partners for Scotland's small business
community. It offers a single point of access to business information,
as well as assistance with business start-up and growth. There are
Small Business Gateway offices throughout Lowland Scotland in:

- Aberdeen
- Aberdeen (Business Information Centre)
- Aboyne
- Alloa
- Arbroath
- Ayr
- Ayrshire (Business Information Centre)
- Clarkston
- Clydebank
- Clydesdale
- Cumbernauld
- Cumnock
- Dalkeith
- Dumbarton
- Dumfries
- Dundee
- East Kilbride
- Edinburgh (Apex House)
- Edinburgh (DHP Scotland Ltd)
- Edinburgh (Edinburgh Chamber of Commerce)
- Falkirk
- Fife - Glenrothes
- Galashiels
- Glasgow (Business Information Centre)
- Glasgow (City Centre)
- Glasgow (West End)
- Govan
- Grangemouth (Business Information Centre)
- Greenock
- Haddington
- Hamilton
- Helensburgh
- Inverurie
- Irvine
- Kilmarnock
- Kirkintilloch
- Livingston
- Milngavie

- Monklands
- Motherwell
- Paisley
- Perth
- Peterhead

- Rutherglen & Cambuslang
- Saltcoats
- Stirling
- Stranraer.

SMALL BUSINESS SERVICE

Kingsgate House, 66-74 Victoria Street, London SW1E 6SW
T: 0845 600 9006
W: www.sbs.gov.uk
[Policy]
SBS is an Executive Agency of the Department of Trade and Industry.
Its policies are implemented throughout the UK by

- England: *Business Link*
- Highland Scotland: *Business Information Service*
- Lowland Scotland: *Small Business Gateway*
- Northern Ireland: *InvestNI*
- Wales: *Business Connect.*

SMALL FIRMS LOAN GUARANTEE SCHEME

W: www.sbs.gov.uk
[Debt]
With effect from 1 April 2003, the SFLGS will:

- Offer a single guarantee rate of 75% for all new loans
- Include Retailing, Catering, Coal, Hairdressing and Beauty Parlours, House and Estate Agents, Libraries, Museums and Cultural Activities, Motor Vehicle Repair and Servicing, Steel and Travel Agents
- Increase the maximum turnover level for non-manufacturing businesses to £3m
- Charge a premium of 2% per year on the outstanding balance for all new loans.
  Applications should be made direct to the lenders, who include:
- *Bank of Ireland* (NI only)
- *Bank of Scotland*
- *Barclays Bank*
- *Clydesdale Bank*
- *Co-operative Bank*
- Doncaster Business Advice Centre

- Emerging Business Trust Ltd
- *First Trust Bank/Allied Irish Banks*
- *HSBC Bank*
- *Lloyds TSB Group*
- *National Westminster Bank*
- *Northern Bank*
- Northern Enterprise Ltd
- Northern Venture Managers Ltd
- oneLondon Ltd
- *Royal Bank of Scotland*
- State Securities PLC
- *Triodos Bank nv*
- *UK Steel Enterprise*
- *Ulster Bank*
- Venture Finance PLC
- *Yorkshire Bank*
- Yorkshire Enterprise Ltd.

SMALLBIZ UK.COM

T: 0113 278 7076 F: 0113 274 8717
E: service@smallbiz.uk.com W: www.smallbiz.uk.com
[Information; Website]
Smallbiz UK works in association with content providers to provide
easy access to practical help for British small firms.

SMALLBUSINESS.CO.UK

T: 0207 430 9777
W: www.smallbusiness.co.uk
[Information; Website]
Sponsored by *Lloyds TSB*, smallbusiness.co.uk provides useful
resources, products and services to help you start and run your own
small business. The site is divided into six key areas of business
decision-making: Starting-Up, Finance, Legal, People, Property and
Sales & Marketing.

SMALLBUSINESSADVICE.ORG.UK

W: smallbusinessadvice.org.uk
[Information; Website]
A free business advice service for pre-start, start-up and small businesses, provided by the *National Federation of Enterprise Agencies.*

SMART

W: www.sbs.gov.uk
[Grants; R&D]
SMART is a SBS (Small Business Service) initiative that promotes innovation by providing grants to help individuals and small and medium-sized enterprises research and develop technologically innovative products and processes. Grants are awarded on a competitive basis. Contact *Business Links* for details.

SMART WALES

W: www.wales.gov.uk/subitradeindustry/content/grantsfor business/smart-e.htm
[Grants; R&D]
SMART is a bi-annual competition offering assistance towards feasibility studies into innovation and technology.

SMART:SCOTLAND

Enterprise and Lifelong Learning Department, The Scottish Executive, 6th Floor, Meridian Court, Cadogan Street, Glasgow G2 6AT
T: 0141 248 4774 F: 0141 242 5665
E: ceu@scotland.gov.uk
W: www.scotland.gov.uk/who/elld/rnd_SMART_1.asp
[Grants; R&D]
The SMART:SCOTLAND competition helps individuals planning to start a business to develop highly innovative products and processes.

SOCIAL ECONOMY AGENCY

45-47 Donegall Street, Belfast BT1 2FG
T: 028 9096 1115 F: 028 9096 1116
2 Bay Road, Derry BT48 7SH
T: 028 7137 1733 F: 028 7137 0114
E: info@socialeconomyagency.org
W: www.socialeconomyagency.org
[**Community & Rural Development; Debt; Grants; Information;
Social Economy; Training**]
The Social Economy Agency provides support to the co-operative
movement in Northern Ireland. It has developed programmes for the
sector, including Capacity Building, New Start, Community Business,
Community Economic Development Initiative (CEDI) and Growth and
Expansion Programmes. A Loan Fund is also available.

SOCIAL ENTERPRISE LONDON

1A Aberdeen Studios, 22-24 Highbury Grove, London N5 2EA
T: 0207 704 7490 F: 0207 704 7499
W: info@sel.org.uk W: www.sel.org.uk
[**Social Economy**]
SEL is tasked with the job of promoting Social Enterprise in London
and increasing the scale of the social economy. Its work involves
improving understanding of Social Enterprise, improving business
support and ensuring access to finance.

SOUTH EAST OF ENGLAND DEVELOPMENT AGENCY

Cross Lanes, Guildford GU1 1YA
T: 01483 484200 F: 01483 484247
E: info@seeda.co.uk W: www.seeda.co.uk
[**Community & Rural Development; Enterprise Support; Grants;
Incubator; Inwards Investment; Policy**]
One of the nine *Regional Development Agencies* established by the
Government in 1999/2000 to promote the sustainable economic
development of the regions. SEEDA works with partners to achieve
sustainable development. It is developing a network of Enterprise
Gateways (with *Business Links*) and Enterprise Hubs (business
incubation units linked to *universities*).

South West Regional Development Agency

Sterling House, Dix's Field, Exeter EX1 1QA
T: 01392 214747 F: 01392 214848
E: enquiries@southwestrda.org.uk W: www.southwestrda.org.uk
[Community & Rural Development; Enterprise Support; Grants; Incubator; Inwards Investment; Policy]
One of the nine *Regional Development Agencies* established by the Government in 1999/2000 to promote the sustainable economic development of the regions. Working through local partners (it has no direct delivery role), the RDA's policies help:

- Regeneration of local communities
- Inward investment
- Business development and support
- Innovation, including incubation and managed workspace.

South Yorkshire Investment Fund

Reresby House, Bow Bridge Close, Rotherham S60 1BY
T: 01709 386377
E: info@syif.com W: www.syif.com
[Business Angels; Debt; Equity; Mentoring]
SYIF offers equity and loan capital to high-growth start-ups and small businesses, as well as a programme and access to a network of private investors and business angels.

Spirit of Enterprise Fund

Northern Enterprise Limited, 3 Earls Court, 5th Avenue Business Park,
Team Valley Trading Estate, Gateshead NE11 0HF
T: 0191 442 4300 F: 0191 442 4301
E: donna.hedley@nel@co.uk
[Debt; Minorities & Disabilities]
A loan fund, up to £5,000, targeted at disabled entrepreneurs in the North East.

Startbusiness.co.uk

PO Box 360,Torquay, Devon TQ1 1XN
E: info@startbusiness.co.uk W: www.startbusiness.co.uk
[Information; Website]
This site is run by experienced start-up advisers, themselves self-employed, for those new to, or contemplating, starting their own business.

StartInBusiness.co.uk

Walker & Gibson Publishing Limited, 53 Head Street,
Colchester, Essex CO1 1NH
W: www.startinbusiness.co.uk
[**Information; Website**]
An online guide to starting a new business.

StartingaBusinessinBritain.com

Oak Tree Press, 19 Rutland Street, Cork, Ireland
T: 00 353 21 431 3855 F: 00 353 21 431 3496
E: info@oaktreepress.com
W: www.startingabusinessinbritain.com
[**Information; Website**]
A source of updates to this **Directory**, as well as other useful
information from an international developer of enterprise training and
support materials.

Startups.co.uk

Crimson Publishing, Gainsborough House, 2 Sheen Road,
Richmond, Surrey TW9 1AE
T: 0208 334 1600 F: 0208 334 1601
W: www.startups.co.uk
[**Information; Website**]
This website provides a wide range of information on starting up and
running your business.

Success4Business

Lloyds TSB PLC, PO Box 65, 2 Brindley Place, Birmingham B1 2AB
T: 0870 900 2069 (help-desk)
E: S4Bhelpdesk@lloydstsb.co.uk W: www.success4business.com
[**Information; Website**]
A free online resource from *Lloyds TSB* that helps registered users to
build and manage their business.

TARGETING TECHNOLOGY LIMITED

Unit 6.08, Kelvin Campus, West of Scotland Science Park,
Glasgow G20 0SP
T: 0141 946 0500 F: 0141 945 1591
E: info@targetingtechnology.co.uk W: targetingtechnology.co.uk
[Mentoring; R&D]
Targeting Technology Ltd helps companies to develop and
commercialise innovative products and processes, and to realise the
worth of their intellectual assets through technology trade and
transfer. It also provides mentoring for client companies. TTL is one of
the partners that deliver *IRC Scotland* services.

TECHNOLOGY VENTURES SCOTLAND

W: www.technologyscotland.org
[R&D]
Technology Ventures Scotland's remit is to commercialise basic
research, thus establishing new businesses and jobs in Scotland.

THE VIRTUAL COMPANY

Business Link Wessex, Wates House, Watlington Hill,
Fareham PO16 7BJ
T: 0845 458 8558 F: 0845 458 8554
E: info@businesslinkwessex.co.uk W: www.blinkdorset.co.uk
[R&D]
The Virtual Company (TVC) is aimed at inventors who wish to
develop their ideas and launch these in the marketplace. During the
collaboration and development process, a virtual company with
virtual shares is formed among the business partners.

THE-BAG-LADY.CO.UK

9 Williams Court, Trade Street, Cardiff CF1 5DQ
T: 029 2034 3703 F: 029 2030 7115
E: inform@the-bag-lady.co.uk W: www.the-bag-lady.co.uk
[Information; Website; Women]
The Bag Lady supports all women business-owners, by providing
information on where to go for a range of business resources. The aim
is a business-one-stop-shop of information.

THE-SME.CO.UK

E: info@the-sme.co.uk W: www.the-sme.co.uk
[Information; Website]
This website is a free resource, aimed at providing easy-to-use
signposting to important and interesting business information and
related services for small and medium-sized enterprises.

TRADE PARTNERS UK

Kingsgate House, 66-74 Victoria Street, London SW1E 6SW
T: 0207 215 5444/5
W: www.tradepartners.gov.uk
[Information]
Trade Partners UK is the lead government organisation for helping
companies based in the UK achieve their export potential. Trade
Partners UK's full range of information, advice and support can be
accessed through Trade Partners UK's local offices throughout the UK
or through the International Trade Teams at 45 *Business Links*
throughout England, *Scottish Development International*, Wales Trade
International or *Invest Northern Ireland*.

TRADENETIRELAND LTD

41 Lisburn Enterprise Centre, Ballinderry Road, Lisburn BT28 2BP
T: 028 9266 1160 F: 028 9260 3084
E: info@tradenetireland.com W: www.tradenetireland.com
[E-Business; Information; Marketing; Website]
TradeNetIreland is an Internet-based business tool designed to
deliver targeted information and trading opportunities to companies
and to encourage SMEs in Northern Ireland (and the Republic) to
access electronic information and participate in electronic commerce.

TRADING STANDARDS INSTITUTE

4/5 Hadleigh Business Centre, 51 London Road, Hadleigh,
Essex S7 2BT
T: 0870 872 9000 F: 0870 872 9025
E: institute@tsi.org.uk W: www.tradingstandards.gov.uk
[Information; Regulator & Standards; Training]
TSI provides consumer protection information in the UK, including
guidance leaflets and training.

TRIODOS BANK

Brunel House, 11 The Promenade, Clifton, Bristol BS8 3NN
T: 0117 973 9339 F: 0117 973 9303
E: mail@triodos.co.uk W: www.triodos.co.uk
[Debt]
Triodos Bank is one of Europe's leading ethical banks and provides
financial solutions for businesses and organisations pursuing positive
social, environmental and cultural goals.

UK BUSINESS INCUBATION

Faraday Wharf, Aston Science Park, Holt Street, Birmingham B7 4BB
T: 0121 250 3538 F: 0121 250 3542
E: info@ukbi.co.uk W: www.ukbi.co.uk
[Incubator; Information; Networking]
UKBI is the national 'voice' of the UK incubation industry, providing
information, advice and networking opportunities as well as events,
research and publications to identify and spread good practice. The
website provides a directory of all incubation facilities in UK.

UK LEADER +

Friars House, 157-168 Blackfriars Road, London SE1 8EZ
T: 0207 803 3160 F: 0207 620 1725
E: W: www.ukleader.org.uk
[Community & Rural Development]
UK LEADER+ Network is the network of LEADER+ Groups in England,
Scotland, Wales and Northern Ireland, which facilitates co-operation
and exchange of experience within in the UK, as well as with the rest
of Europe. LEADER+ Groups in the UK include:

- Adventa
- Argyll, Isles & Lochaber L+
- Blackdown Hills
- Cadwyn Clwyd
- Cairngorms LEADER+
- Coleraine Local Action Group for Enterprise Ltd
- Craigavon & Armagh Rural Development
- Cumbria Fells and Dales LEADER+
- Dorset Chalk & Cheese LEADER+
- Dumfries & Galloway L+
- East Fife LEADER+
- East Riding of Yorkshire L+

- East Tyrone LEADER+
- Fenland LeAP
- Fermanagh Local Action Group
- Glasu
- Herefordshire Rivers LEADER+
- Isle of Wight Rural Action Zone LEADER+
- L+ Peak, Dales & Moorlands
- Lancashire L+
- Lincolnshire Fenland
- Lomond & Rural Stirling LEADER+
- Magherafelt Area Partnership Ltd
- Menter Môn
- Mid Kent L+
- Moray Community Action LEADER+
- New Forest LEADER+
- Newry & Mourne LEADER
- Norfolk Broads & Rivers LEADER+
- North Antrim LEADER Ltd
- North Highland L+ (Heritage)
- North Highland L+ (youth) Partnership
- North Northumberland LEADER+
- North Pennines LEADER+
- North West Devon
- Northern Isles L+ (Orkney)
- Northern Isles L+ (Shetland)
- Northern Marches – Eng LEADER+
- Northern Marches Cymru LEADER+
- Penistone
- PLANED
- RAPID
- Rockingham Forest
- Roe Valley Rural Development Ltd
- Rural Conwy
- Rural Down LEADER+
- Rural Tayside LEADER+ Prog
- Scottish Borders LEADER+
- Selby LEADER+
- Somerset Level & Moors LEADER+

- South Antrim LEADER+
- South Lanarkshire
- Sustain the Plain LEADER+
- Teignbridge
- Tyne/Esk LEADER+
- Tyne/Esk LEADER+
- WARR LEADER+
- Wealden and Rother LEADER+
- West Oxfordshire Network
- West Tyrone LEADER+
- Western Isles, Skye & Lochalsh

UK ONLINE

W: www.ukonline.gov.uk
[Information; Website]
This website is a first port of call for intending British entrepreneurs. It provides a range of useful information, as well as a start-up pack.

UK SCIENCE PARK ASSOCIATION

Aston Science Park, Love Lane, Birmingham B7 4BJ
T: 0121 359 0981 F: 0121 333 5852
E: admin.ukspa@btconnect.com W: www.ukspa.org.uk
[R&D]
The authoritative body on the planning, development and operation of Science Parks in the UK.

UK STEEL ENTERPRISE LTD

The Innovation Centre, 217 Portobello, Sheffield S1 4DP
T: 0114 273 1612 F: 0114 270 1390
E: ho@uksteelenterprise.co.uk W: www.uksteelenterprise.co.uk
[Debt; Equity]
UK Steel Enterprise is the subsidiary of Corus Group PLC whose mission is to help in the economic development of those areas of the UK affected by changes in the steel industry. It can provide premises, loans, share capital, or a combination, to small businesses with growth potential, engaged in manufacturing or related service activities and located in UK Steel operating areas.

ULSTER BANK

11-16 Donegall Square East, Belfast BT1 5UB
T: 028 9027 6017 F: 028 9027 6033
[Debt]
Ulster Bank, a member of the *Royal Bank of Scotland* Group, has a
Small Business Adviser in every branch to guide entrepreneurs
through the start-up process. Its Franchise Unit provides support to
both franchisers and franchisees. Its website explains the '7 Steps to
Starting up a Business'.

UNIVERSITIES

[Incubator; R&D; Start-Up Training; Training]
Most UK universities provide support to entrepreneurs ranging from
training through to incubation facilities – inquire locally. UK
universities include:

- Anglia Polytechnic University W: www.anglia.ac.uk
- Aston University W: www.aston.ac.uk
- Birkbeck College [Part of the University of London]
  W: www.bbk.ac.uk
- Bournemouth University W: www.bournemouth.ac.uk
- Brunel University W:www.brunel.ac.uk
- Cardiff University W: www.cardiff.ac.uk
- City University W: www.city.ac.uk
- Coventry University W: www.coventry.ac.uk
- Cranfield University W: www.cranfield.ac.uk
- De Montfort University W: www.dmu.ac.uk
- Glasgow Caledonian University W: www.gcal.ac.uk
- Goldsmiths College [Part of the University of London]
  W: www.goldsmiths.ac.uk
- Heriot-Watt University W: www.hw.ac.uk
- Imperial College of Science, Technology and Medicine [Part of the
  University of London] W: www.imperial.ac.uk
- Keele University W: www.keele.ac.uk
- Kings College London [Part of the University of London]
  W: www.kcl.ac.uk
- Kingston University W: www.kingston.ac.uk
- Leeds Metropolitan University W: www.lmu.ac.uk
- Liverpool John Moores University W: www.livjm.ac.uk

- London Business School [Part of the University of London] W: www.london.edu
- London Metropolitan University W: www.londonmet.ac.uk
- London School of Economics and Political Science [Part of the University of London] W: www.lse.ac.uk
- Loughborough University W: www.lboro.ac.uk
- Manchester Metropolitan University W: www.mmu.ac.uk
- Middlesex University W: www.mdx.ac.uk
- Napier University W: www.napier.ac.uk
- Nottingham Trent University W: www.ntu.ac.uk
- Open University W: www.open.ac.uk
- Oxford Brookes University W: www.brookes.ac.uk
- Queen Margaret University College W: www.qmuc.ac.uk
- Queen's University of Belfast W: www.qub.ac.uk
- Robert Gordon University W: www.rgu.ac.uk
- Sheffield Hallam University W: www.shu.ac.uk
- South Bank University W: www.sbu.ac.uk
- Staffordshire University W: www.staffs.ac.uk
- Thames Valley University W: www.tuv.ac.uk
- Trinity College, Cambridge W: www.trinity-cm.ac.uk
- University College London [Part of the University of London] W: www.ucl.ac.uk
- University of Aberdeen W: www.abdn.ac.uk
- University of Abertay Dundee W: www.abertay.ac.uk
- University of Bath W: www.bath.ac.uk
- University of Birmingham W: www.bham.ac.uk
- University of Bradford W: www.bradford.ac.uk
- University of Brighton W: www.brighton.ac.uk
- University of Bristol W: www.bristol.ac.uk
- University of Buckingham W: www.buckingham.ac.uk
- University of Cambridge W: www.cam.ac.uk
- University of Central England in Birmingham W: www.uce.ac.uk
- University of Central Lancashire W: www.uclan.ac.uk
- University of Derby W: www.derby.ac.uk
- University of Dundee W: www.dundee.ac.uk
- University of Durham W: www.dur.ac.uk
- University of East Anglia W: www.uea.ac.uk
- University of East London W: www.uel.ac.uk

- University of Edinburgh W: www.ed.ac.uk
- University of Essex W: www.essex.ac.uk
- University of Exeter W: www.ex.ac.uk
- University of Glamorgan W: www.glam.ac.uk
- University of Glasgow W: www.gla.ac.uk
- University of Gloucestershire W: www.glos.ac.uk
- University of Greenwich W: www.greenwich.ac.uk
- University of Hertfordshire W: www.herts.ac.uk
- University of Huddersfield W: www.hud.ac.uk
- University of Hull W: www.hull.ac.uk
- University of Kent W: www.ukc.ac.uk
- University of Lancaster W: www.lancs.ac.uk
- University of Leeds W: www.leeds.ac.uk
- University of Leicester W: www.le.ac.uk
- University of Lincoln W: www.lincoln.ac.uk
- University of Liverpool W: www.liv.ac.uk
- University of London W: www.lon.ac.uk
- University of Luton W: www.luton.ac.uk
- University of Manchester W: www.man.ac.uk
- University of Manchester Institute of Science & Technology
  W: www.umist.ac.uk
- University of Newcastle W: www.ncl.ac.uk
- University of Northumbria at Newcastle W: www.unn.ac.uk
- University of Nottingham W: www.nottingham.ac.uk
- University of Oxford W: www.ox.ac.uk
- University of Paisley W: www.paisley.ac.uk
- University of Plymouth W: www.plymouth.ac.uk
- University of Portsmouth W: www.port.ac.uk
- University of Reading W: www.reading.ac.uk
- University of Salford W: www.salford.ac.uk
- University of Sheffield W: www.shef.ac.uk
- University of Southampton W: www.soton.ac.uk
- University of St Andrews W: www.st-and.ac.uk
- University of Stirling W: www.stir.ac.uk
- University of Strathclyde W: www.strath.ac.uk
- University of Sunderland W: www.sunderland.ac.uk
- University of Surrey W: www.surrey.ac.uk
- University of Surrey Roehampton W: www.roehampton.ac.uk

- University of Sussex W: www.sussex.ac.uk
- University of Teesside W: www.tees.ac.uk
- University of the West of England, Bristol W: www.uwe.ac.uk
- University of Ulster W: www.ulster.ac.uk
- University of Wales W: www.aber.ac.uk
- University of Wales College, Newport [Part of the University of Wales] W: www.newport.ac.uk
- University of Wales Institute, Cardiff [Part of the University of Wales] W: www.uwic.ac.uk
- University of Wales, Aberystwyth [Part of the University of Wales] W: www.aber.ac.uk
- University of Wales, Bangor [Part of the University of Wales] W: www.bangor.ac.uk
- University of Wales, Lampeter [Part of the University of Wales] W: www.lamp.ac.uk
- University of Wales, Swansea [Part of the University of Wales] W: www.swan.ac.uk
- University of Warwick W: www.warwick.ac.uk
- University of Westminster W: www.wmin.ac.uk
- University of Wolverhampton W: www.wlv.ac.uk
- University of York W: www.york.ac.uk.

UUTECH LTD

University of Ulster, Cromore Road,
Coleraine, Co Londonderry BT52 1SA
T: 028 7032 4445 F: 028 7032 3028
E: cr.barnett@ulst.ac.uk W: www.ulst.ac.uk/uusrp
[Grants; Incubator; Intellectual Property]
The University of Ulster established UUTech Ltd to implement and develop its technology and knowledge transfer policy. Services available to entrepreneurs from UUTech include structured business development, finance, information on grants, awards and links with local development agencies, accommodation and technical support.

WALES SPINOUT PROGRAMME

W: www.spinoutwales.co.uk
[R&D]
The Wales Spinout Programme helps new businesses 'spinout' from
Universities and Higher Education Institutes in Wales, providing a
Spinout Manager to support and assist the new business.

WELLPARK ENTERPRISE CENTRE

120 Sydney Street, Glasgow G31 1JF
T: 0141 550 4994 F: 0141 550 4443
E: info@wellpark.co.uk W: www.wellpark.co.uk
[Training; Women]
Wellpark Enterprise Centre is 'a centre of excellence committed to
the growth and development of women in business'.

WELSH ASSEMBLY

See *National Assembly of Wales.*

WELSH DEVELOPMENT AGENCY

Plas Glyndwr, Kingsway, Cardiff CF10 3AH
T: 01443 845500 F: 01443 845589
E: enquiries@wda.co.uk W: www.wda.co.uk
[Enterprise Support; Information; Inwards Investment; Website]
The WDA is the lead enabler of business support in Wales. The
Entrepreneurship Action Plan is a long-term economic programme by
the National Assembly for Wales and is being delivered through
partnerships involving the WDA, private, public and voluntary sector
organisations. See also *Business Connect Wales.*

WEST MIDLANDS FINANCE

W: www.westmidlandsfinance.com
[Debt; Equity; Grants; Information; Website]
Provided by *Advantage West Midlands*, this website offers information
and advice on obtaining different types of finance, as well as a
searchable database of grants, asset finance and cash flow finance
providers, venture capitalists, business angel networks, banks, cash
awards and soft loans available to SMEs in the West Midlands.

WHICHFRANCHISE.COM

78 Carlton Place, Glasgow, G5 9TH
T: 0141 429 5900 F: 0141 429 5901
E: info@whichfranchise.com W: www.whichfranchise.com
[**Franchises; Information; Website**]
Affiliated to the *British Franchise Association*, the website provides a
self-test of your suitability for franchising, as well other information on
franchising and franchises available for purchase.

WOMEN MEAN BUSINESS AWARDS

Stable Yard, 16 Balham Hill, London SW12 9EB
T: 0208 673 2020
[**Competitions; Women**]
The Awards, presented in association with the **Sunday Express**, are a
national search to find Britain's top, self-made businesswomen, with
£40,000 of cash and prizes waiting for the winners.

YORKSHIRE BANK PLC

20 Merrion Way, Leeds LS2 8NZ
W: www.ybonline.co.uk
[**Debt**]
Yorkshire Bank is a member of the National Australia Bank Group,
which includes *Clydesdale Bank*, *National Irish Bank* and *Northern
Bank*.

YORKSHIRE FORWARD
(REGIONAL DEVELOPMENT AGENCY FOR YORKSHIRE & THE HUMBER REGION)

Victoria House, Victoria Place, Leeds LS11 5AE
T: 0113 394 9600
W: www.yorkshire-forward.com
[**Community & Rural Development; Enterprise Support; Grants;
Incubator; Inwards Investment; Policy**]
One of the nine *Regional Development Agencies* established by the
Government in 1999/2000 to promote the sustainable economic
development of the regions. Yorkshire Forward attracts inward
investment and jobs into the region, funds community-based
regeneration schemes and promotes business development
generally.

Young Company Finance

T: 0131 315 4443
E: jonathan@ycf.co.uk W: www.youngcompanyfinance.co.uk
[Business Angels; Information; Publications]
Young Company Finance is a monthly newsletter that covers early-stage high growth companies in Scotland. It regularly profiles venture capitalists and business angels.

Young Enterprise

Peterley House, Peterley Road, Oxford OX2 2TZ
T: 01865 776845 F: 01865 775671
W: www.young-enterprise.org.uk
[Competitions; Young Enterprise]
Young Enterprise delivers vocational training programmes in entrepreneurship and economic literacy to the 15-25 plus age group. See also *Young Enterprise Scotland* and *Young Enterprise Northern Ireland.*

Young Enterprise Northern Ireland

Unit 11, Curran House, 155 Northumberland Street, Belfast BT13 2JF
T: 028 9032 7003 F: 028 9032 6995
W: www.yeni.co.uk
[Competitions; Young Enterprise]
Young Enterprise delivers vocational training programmes in entrepreneurship and economic literacy to the 15-25 plus age group. See also *Young Enterprise and Young Enterprise Scotland.*

Young Enterprise Scotland

Graham Hills Building, 50 George Street, Glasgow G1 1BA
T: 0141 548 4930 F: 0141 548 4940
E: support@yes.org.uk W: www.yes.org.uk
[Competitions; Young Enterprise]
Young Enterprise Scotland delivers vocational training programmes in entrepreneurship and economic literacy to the 15-25 plus age group. It has achieved 75% penetration of all schools in Scotland, delivering the YES programme to over 5,000 young people. See also *Young Enterprise.*

Your People Manager

3 Waterhouse Square, 142 Holborn, London EC1N 2NX
T: 0207 961 0300
E: feedback@yourpeoplemanager.com
W: www.yourpeoplemanager.com
[Training]
YPM is a new service from *Investors in People UK*, aimed at helping the managers of small businesses deal with the everyday questions, issues and problems of managing staff.